PRAISE FOR GREEN LIVING HANDBOOK

"A movement . . . of unquestionable zeal is challenging consumption at the grass-roots . . . local support groups called EcoTeams are methodically helping members reduce the amount and kind of material that flows in and out of homes."
The New York Times

"The process works even for those who consider themselves hard-core environmentalists. A senior sales executive and an EcoTeam member says, 'As a result of the awareness the group has brought us, we all have changed our consumption habits and our lifestyles, in the products we purchase, and the utilities we use'."
The Philadelphia Inquirer

"EcoTeams help people build community while working toward something they believe in. It takes a village to save the Earth."
Family Circle

"The biggest thing about EcoTeams is that they are helping people change behavior. You could do information campaigns and hope people change, but as a city, this is a better investment."
The Kansas City Star

"This program is skillfully designed to be attractive to individuals, local governments, and businesses . . . It has demonstrated results . . . it can make a real difference. In our work with communities across America, this is exactly the sort of tool for which they are searching."
Molly Olson, Executive Director, President's Council on Sustainable Development (Clinton Administration)

"The *Green Living Handbook* is excellent. An enormous amount of time and work went into producing it. Congratulations on a superb job."
Denis Hayes, Co-founder Earth Day, President and CEO, Bullitt Foundation

"The EcoTeam approach opens up a new category of policy instruments having to do with voluntary change. The program is more sophisticated than information campaigns, since it gives people the personal support they need to change their ingrained habits of how they use resources."
Paul de Jongh, Deputy Director General for Environmental Protection, The Netherlands, Author, Dutch "Green Plan".

"The *Green Living Handbook* is unique and effective."
Honorable Maurice Hinchey, Committee on Natural Resources, Congress of the United States

"The *Green Living Handbook* is a highly effective new tool for environmental protection. We see it as a significant opportunity to achieve citizen behavior change which has been one of our most difficult challenges in advancing environmental protection. The program couldn't be more timely."
Lang Marsh, Director, Oregon Department of Environmental Quality

"We are all optimistic here. You have the entire household involved in a voluntary way instead of having a program that is mandated by the government. This is at the most grassroots level possible, and that makes it more effective."
Mike Lindberg, City Council Member and Commissioner of Public Utilities, City of Portland, OR

"The Environmental Services Department has researched multiple programs and approaches to provide the desired proactive waste prevention education. *Green Living Handbook* was the only program that successfully produced measurable resource savings and sustained behavior change."
Alisa Wade, Environmental Services Department, City of San Jose, CA

"The potential resource savings are tremendous . . . and what's truly exciting about the EcoTeam approach is that it can serve as a catalyst to creating a more sustainable community."
Ava Frisinger, Mayor, City of Issaquah, WA

"I had thought about all the things I should do and talked about doing them before the program; but it took the *Green Living Handbook* and group support to turn my thinking and talking into specific and concrete actions. And the changes were relatively easy."
Pat Spindel, St. Louis, MO

"I feel this program is superb, not only because of what it has done for me, but because it has the potential to do so much for the community."
Krista M. Schauer, Portland, OR

"I've lived in the neighborhood for 21 years, but getting to know my neighbors started three years ago with an EcoTeam. We knew a lot of people by sight, but now we know them much better. There is a lot more friendliness on the streets now. It's given us the feeling of being embedded in the community and having roots. I highly recommend the neighborhood EcoTeam process."
Sarah Conn, West Newton, MA

"When you put things in small, workable chunks as the *Green Living Handbook* has done here, it's easier for people to accomplish things and follow through."
Maria Sichel, Medway, MA

MIAMI DADE COLLEGE
Hialeah Campus Library
1780 West 49th Street
Room 1116
Hialeah, Florida 33012
(305) 237-8722

GREEN LIVING HANDBOOK

A 6 Step Program to Create an Environmentally Sustainable Lifestyle

David Gershon

Saving the Planet . . . One Household at a Time

DEDICATION

This book is dedicated to the future generations to whom we are bequeathing our Earth. May we rise to the occasion and offer them the beauty we have seen.

SPECIAL THANKS

Andrea Barrist Stern, Robert Gilman and Eve Baer for their invaluable collaboration in helping create prior editions of this book. Dan Wetzel for his charming illustrations that help make the journey to a greener life more fun. Steve Busch for his graphic artistry and cover design. Craig Hamilton for his skillful editorial assistance. My Global Action Plan colleagues for their great work getting this program in the hands of tens of thousands of people around the world. Margo Baldwin and Peg O'Donnell of Chelsea Green for their partnership and vast publishing wisdom. Joe Laur, Ben Bassi and the Greenopolis team for their collaboration in getting the book out through their wonderful website. The many people who have gone through the program and provided feedback that has helped improve it over the years. Lastly my wife Gail Straub, the love of my life, for her kind and loving support of me on this life journey.

All rights reserved. No part of this book may be reproduced or transmitted in any form or by any means, electronic or mechanical including photocopying, recording or by any information storage and retrieval system without written permission from Empowerment Institute, except where permitted by law.

ISBN 978-0-9630327-4-4
Copyright © 2008 David Gershon
Third Edition
10 9 8 7 6 5 4 3 2 1
This is a new and expanded edition.
The previous edition was called EcoTeam.
Printed in Canada

Published by:
Empowerment Institute
P.O. Box 428
Woodstock, New York 12498

www.empowermentinstitute.net

This book is printed on 100% post consumer waste
Forest Stewardship Certified recycled paper, using plant-based inks.
The paper is processed chlorine free and manufactured using biogas energy.

By using 100% post consumer waste recycled paper instead of virgin fibers,
this edition saved:

Trees: 50
Solid waste: 3,159lb
Water: 29,818gal
Suspended particles in the water: 20.0lb
Air emissions: 6,937lb
Natural gas: 7,229ft³

It's the equivalent of:
Tree(s): 1 football field
Water: a shower of 6.3 days
Air emissions: emissions of 0.6 cars per year

The following results represent the reported feedback from over 20,000 participants in this program. The percentages reflect annual average savings.

- 40% less garbage sent into the waste stream

- 32% less water used

- 14% less energy used

- 18% less fuel used for transportation

- 15% less CO_2 emissions

- and a financial savings of $255

all while improving their quality of life!

"Never doubt that a small group of committed individuals can change the world - indeed, it's the only thing that ever has."

– Margaret Mead

Team Purpose Statement:

_____

_____

_____

_____

_____

TABLE OF CONTENTS

Step 4: Ticket to Ride - Transportation Efficiency

Step 5: Good Buys Are Forever - Eco-wise Consuming

Step 6: You Make the Difference - Empowering Others

Sustainable Lifestyle Assessment

Program Support Tools

SAVING THE PLANET...
ONE HOUSEHOLD AT A TIME

You are about to embark on a great adventure, one that will enable you to use our Earth's precious and limited resources with greater care. It will be exciting, sometimes challenging and definitely full of meaning. With the help of this handbook you will learn how to develop environmentally sustainable lifestyle practices. *Sustainable* means using the Earth's resources (trees, water, energy, minerals, etc.) in a way that makes sure there will be enough for others - today and tomorrow.

A term that aptly describes this approach is *stewardship*. Webster defines steward as "one called to exercise responsible care over possessions entrusted to him or her." This program will enable you to be a responsible steward of the Earth's resources you use. It will enhance your quality of life and provide financial savings. It will also offer you a rich experience of community. Perhaps its greatest benefit though, will be the personal satisfaction you receive from making a tangible contribution to our children's future.

The United Nations plan for restoring the environment, "Agenda 21", states: "The major cause of the continued deterioration of the global environment is the unsustainable patterns of consumption and production particularly in the industrialized countries." It calls on the developed countries "to take the lead in achieving sustainable consumption."

As 5% of the world's population, America uses a third of the planet's resources and wastes up to 75% through inefficiency and lack of awareness. Since 35% of these resources are directly consumed by households and the rest are influenced by our shopping practices, the lifestyle choices we make are significant. America's adoption of more environmentally sustainable lifestyles is a major part of the solution.

Tens of thousands of households throughout the world have participated in this program in over twenty countries. I hope countless more will participate in the future. Thanks for doing your part. Go to the next page, follow the instructions and enjoy the journey for a lifetime. I wish you well.

HOW THE PROGRAM WORKS

1. Using this handbook, you take action to develop sustainable lifestyle practices in five areas: garbage, water, energy, transportation, and consumption. The sixth action area, empowerment enables you to help others take action for the planet.

2. You can do this program either with your household family members or as part of a peer support group of friends, neighbors, co-workers, or members of your faith community or civic organization - an EcoTeam. A good size for an EcoTeam is 5 to 8 households. Doing it with other households is recommended as it strengthens motivation to complete the actions and is a lot of fun.

3. In either format, the program is designed to be completed in 7 meetings that take place every 14 days to 2 weeks. Different team members run the meetings using scripts located in the support section of this handbook. Meetings last 1.5 to 2 hours, with several hours needed between meetings to take the selected actions. If you do the program as an individual household and live with others, turn your household members into an EcoTeam and adapt the meeting scripts accordingly. If you live alone and choose to do this on your own, use the program's suggested time sequence to keep you motivated.

4. In the team program, the first meeting - Team Building Meeting - you review each of the program elements, build a team, schedule the remaining meetings and choose people to lead them. During meetings 2 to 7, team participants report on actions taken and describe their action plans for the next section. The team provides support and inspiration for everyone to carry out their plans.

5. Before each meeting, read all the actions from the related handbook pages, fill in that chapter's Sustainable Lifestyle Assessment (Section 7) and decide which actions you will take. Then transfer your "will do" actions to the Action Log in the beginning of each section and decide when you will take the actions. If you live with others, discuss your plan with them to get their ideas and participation.

6. Each action you take has a point value based on effort or resources saved. To keep track of your accomplishments, after you have done each action, check it off on your Action Log and fill in the "after program" column of the Sustainable Lifestyle Assessment.

7. Participate in our Green Living on-line community to exchange ideas with others doing the program, add your results to our sustainability scorecard, and take advantage of additional program resources. Visit www.greenopolis.com/glh

That's it! Have fun as you improve life on our planet.

DUMPING ON GARBAGE—ACTION LOG

Actions	Action Plan		Discussed with Household	Action Done	Points
Back by Popular Demand	Day:	Time:	☐	☐	3
Bag Bags	Day:	Time:	☐	☐	2
Bring Your Own	Day:	Time:	☐	☐	3
Two Sides Are Better Than One	Day:	Time:	☐	☐	1
Junk Mail Diet	Day:	Time:	☐	☐	3
Let It Rot	Day:	Time:	☐	☐	3
Wipe Swipe	Day:	Time:	☐	☐	2
A-Mend	Day:	Time:	☐	☐	3
Trash or Treasure	Day:	Time:	☐	☐	2
Celebrate with the Earth in Mind	Day:	Time:	☐	☐	1
Poop Scoop	Day:	Time:	☐	☐	4
Cut It High and Let It Lie	Day:	Time:	☐	☐	4
Relating to Nature: Roots	Day:	Time:	☐	☐	1
Farther Down the Path: A Zero Garbage Household	Day:	Time:	☐	☐	6

STEP 1 DUMPING ON GARBAGE
REDUCING YOUR SOLID WASTE

GARBAGE AND YOU

There is no such thing as garbage in nature. Everything nature creates is used to create something else. This is not how human beings currently operate, and we are beginning to discover the consequences of our mistaken notion called garbage.

There are ever fewer places for our garbage to go because of community opposition to local landfill sitings and incinerators. When a new landfill is sited, many people believe it will eventually leak into the groundwater and have to be reclaimed in the future at significant environmental and financial expense. This confrontation with reality is forcing us to change our notion of garbage. Garbage is an idea whose time is going.

The new motto for a responsible global citizen is What I bring into my house I steward. Accepting this maxim asks us to think carefully before we step into the role of stewarding something. The question, Do I have a way to reuse or recycle this object? needs to be part of our basic approach to using the Earth's resources.

This section will help you develop the necessary lifestyle practices to more effectively steward the resources you bring into your home. Perhaps you can be the first on your block to have a no-garbage household — a challenge indeed, but one that must eventually become commonplace if we are to create a sustainable planet. See it as an adventure and have fun with it!

BACK BY POPULAR DEMAND
RECYCLING

 WHY ACT? The average American generates about 4.6 pounds of garbage per day. It is becoming increasingly difficult to site new landfills or incinerators, but there is something you can do. Through careful recycling, you can reduce the amount of garbage you send into the waste stream by 50% to 75% or more! This Earth Action will show you how to create a recycling center in your home.

EARTH ACTION
• Get sorting guidelines from your local recycling center or trash collection service.
• Set up bags, boxes, or bins (your household recycling center) according to these guidelines.
• Show the members of your household where things go.
• Separate all your recyclables; compost all organic waste. (See "Let It Rot" p. 10)
• If your city or town does not have a pickup service, take your recyclables to the recycling center.
• If your community is not already recycling, encourage them to start.

MATERIALS
• Bags, boxes, or bins; markers; transportation.

TIME
• 30 minutes for setup.

RESOURCE SAVINGS

You save sending your garbage on a permanent trip to the landfill or incinerator, and become a participant in one of nature's most remarkable processes: recycling!

ME! ME!

NO, ME!

ANY FOR ME, PLEASE?

CANS   CLEAR GLASS   NEWSPAPERS

BAG BAGS

RE-USING BAGS

WHY ACT? How many paper and plastic bags do you end up with after a week of routine shopping? 10 or 12? Probably even more if you consider the supermarket and specialty food stores, the drug store, and all the other stops on your shopping trips. Don't forget lunches and take-outs and all the miscellaneous things that enter your home in bags. That's a lot of paper and plastic. This Earth Action will show you a simple alternative that will make you feel good every time you do it.

RESOURCE SAVINGS

Saving paper saves trees. Two bags per day amounts to over 700 bags per year. By not using paper bags, you can save the equivalent of one 15-year-old tree. Not using plastic bags saves oil. You also lessen the need for energy to produce them and resources to manage the waste if they are not recycled. Your effort made a difference for that 15 year-old tree!

EARTH ACTION

- Assemble a supply of cloth bags or a backpack. (See "Bring Your Own" p. 7, for other ideas for these bags.)
- Keep your bags in a convenient place, like the car. A string or nylon bag tucks away conveniently in a pocketbook, briefcase, or backpack. After you bring the bags home and empty them, make sure you leave them by the door so you will remember to take them with you the next time you go shopping.
- This action is not just about knowing what to do; it's about remembering to do it. Tailor it to your own lifestyle.
- You may need to educate the people serving you so they understand why you are bringing your own bag(s). Next time the store clerk asks, "Paper or plastic?" bring out your own, smile, and say, "Cloth!"

MATERIALS

- Cloth bags or backpacks.

TIME

- A few minutes to buy or make your cloth bags; a few seconds to use them.

BRING YOUR OWN
RE-USING CONTAINERS

Packaging accounts for up to a third of the garbage you send into the waste stream every year. Much of this paper, plastic, and Styrofoam isn't easily recycled. Also, resources were needed to manufacture packaging the first time and will be needed again for the recycling process. This Earth Action will help you reduce much of the packaging you bring into your house and send out into the environment.

EARTH ACTION
• Create a BYO kit by putting some reusable, durable containers in a cloth bag or a backpack. (See "Bag Bags" p. 6.) Use them for food take-out, bulk food purchases, and doggie bags. Include a covered mug for take-out coffee, tea, or soda; flatware; and a cloth napkin.
• Remember to keep your kit in a convenient place like the car, if you have one. After using it, put it by the door so you'll take it with you the next time.

MATERIALS
• Reusable, durable containers; plastic covered mug; flatware; cloth napkin; cloth bag or backpack.

TIME
• Half an hour to assemble your kit; little extra time to use it; a few minutes to wash and repack the items.

RESOURCE SAVINGS

You lessen the demand for trees and energy that would have been needed to produce the packaging. Your common sense serves as an inspiration to others!

BOB'S Take Out

This tastes great!

Try Some of mine!

TWO SIDES ARE BETTER THAN ONE

USING BOTH SIDES OF PAPER

 WHY ACT? How often do we discard a piece of paper that still has an unused side left? That's half its life. This Earth Action will help you reduce your use of paper by getting you in the habit of using both sides.

EARTH ACTION

- Identify the uses for paper in your home and daily life, such as letters, directions, homework, drawings, shopping lists, phone messages, doodles, etc.
- Note the places where you or other household members normally do this writing or drawing.
- In each of these locations, stack paper that has a blank side, including junk mail. Cut the paper to the appropriate size for that use and, if necessary, draw an X across the used side to prevent confusion.
- Consider also recycling manila and other envelopes by placing clean labels over the old addresses.

MATERIALS

- Partially used paper and junk mail; boxes; scissors; pen; labels.

TIME

- 15 minutes to create your "paper trail."

RESOURCE SAVINGS

Reusing paper lessens the demand for trees and resources required to manage the waste and produce the paper. Your modest effort goes a long way!

JUNK MAIL DIET

REDUCING JUNK MAIL

 WHY ACT? This year, you will spend about 16 hours—or the equivalent of two working days—sorting through your junk mail and only opening a little more than half. This Earth Action will help you avoid having most of this junk mail sent to you in the first place. Enjoy the extra time!

EARTH ACTION

- To reduce junk mail, visit one of these websites, which offer various options for having your name removed from direct marketing lists: www.greendimes.com; www.dmachoice.org/MPS/mps_consumer_description.php; http://www.newdream.org/junkmail/. This should eliminate most of your junk mail.
- Contact those companies whose catalogs you still want and make them aware your name is listed with the Mail Preference Service. Ask them to keep your name on their "in-house" list only and not to sell your name to other companies.
- Above your address label on the junk mail you do receive, write a message stating that you would like to be taken off the company's mailing list. You can return your message in the company's own self-addressed, postage-paid envelope.
- Ask your post office not to put advertising circulars in your mailbox or post office box. Be diligent. Write the local postmaster if necessary.
- Recycle whatever junk mail you do receive, and use the blank backs of pages as scrap paper.

MATERIALS

- Stamps and envelopes, if not provided.

TIME

- A few minutes each time you collect the mail until you're only getting the mail you want.
- It is recommended that you do this every six months.

RESOURCE SAVINGS

If you eliminate all the junk mail you receive in a year, you can lessen the demand for one and a half trees being used and save resources needed to manage the waste. That's "f-i-r-s-t c-l-a-s-s!"

LET IT ROT

COMPOSTING

Food left on plates after a meal and cooking scraps are garbage only if you treat them that way! A quarter of your household waste is composed of organic materials that could be composted instead of buried in landfills. Composting, a process that turns your kitchen and yard wastes into choice fertilizer, can be used to enrich garden soil. A compost pile can be as simple and cost-free as the recipe below or as state-of-the-art as a store-bought composter. This Earth Action will show you how to assist nature in her magic.

RESOURCE SAVINGS

If you compost your food and yard wastes, you can reduce what you send to a landfill by approximately 25%. And if you have a garden, you can eliminate the need for chemical fertilizer. You are a player in Nature's wonder!

EARTH ACTION

- Build a compost pile or purchase a composter.
- If you decide to build your own, check your local laws for guidelines. Here's one method:
  ✓ Put a layer of sticks 3 feet long and 3 feet wide on the ground.
  ✓ Add a 2-3-inch layer of dry brown leaves or soil.
  ✓ Add a 2-3-inch layer of grass clippings, if you have them.
  ✓ Dig a hole in the middle of your mound and drop in your leftovers.
  ✓ Cover the hole with soil, yard waste, or a plastic tarp to discourage animals from having a picnic.
  ✓ Stir and turn it with a pitchfork or shovel every week or so.
  ✓ Water your compost lightly several days a week to speed up the decomposition process.
- Set a bucket with a tight-fitting lid next to your dishwashing and cooking area.
- After every meal, scrape your compostable nonmeat, nondairy, nonoily leftovers into the bucket and close it tight.
- Every few days—or when it's full—take your scrap bucket outside and add the contents to your compost pile.
- It's OK if you don't have all of these materials. Just about anything that comes from plants will turn back into soil in time.
- You can compost in a city or apartment using very tightly-sealed garbage bags stored in a warm place. Not the squeamish sort? Then compost using a worm bucket. Ask your local plant nursery for more details.

MATERIALS

- Food scraps, sticks, and yard waste; bucket and lid; or a store-bought composter.

TIME

- About one hour for setup and a few minutes every few days for care.

WIPE SWIPE
USING CLOTH INSTEAD OF PAPER

Paper napkins may seem inexpensive and convenient, but they have their environmental cost. If you use two napkins per day, that's over 700 each year. It could be more if you factor in your coffee breaks, snacks, and the wad of napkins restaurants sometimes stuff in with your take-out order. Tissues and paper towels—as well as the boxes and packaging they require—are another needless waste of paper and energy. This Earth Action will help you make the pleasurable transition from paper to cloth.

EARTH ACTION
- Set the table with cloth napkins. The money you save at the market by not buying paper products should more than enable you to purchase some additional everyday cloth napkins if necessary.
- Keep dish towels in the kitchen at all times.
- Get in the habit of using dish towels, sponges, rags, and old clothes for jobs where you once used paper, like washing windows and mopping up spills. Use a cloth towel to dry your hands. At last, a way to make the single sock syndrome work to our advantage!
- Substitute handkerchiefs for tissues.

MATERIALS
- Cloth napkins; dish towels and hand towels; handkerchiefs; sponges; rags.

TIME
- A few minutes to rummage through your closets and drawers for the materials, or to buy some cloth napkins, towels, or handkerchiefs.

RESOURCE SAVINGS

Saving paper lessens the demand for trees and energy. It also saves resources needed to manage the waste as well as the toxic chemicals generally used in the manufacture of paper.

A-MEND

REPAIRING ITEMS INSTEAD OF THROWING THEM AWAY

 If you take an inventory of personal or household items not being used because they need repair, the results might surprise you. This Earth Action will help you breathe new life into a lot of unused items. Consider this action especially for large bulky items that have greater impact on landfills.

RESOURCE SAVINGS

For every item you repair, you lessen the demand for resources to produce a similar item. Allow yourself to feel a sense of pride for everything you mend instead of throw away.

EARTH ACTION

- Make an inventory of the personal or household items that are broken or need repair.
- Separate what can realistically be repaired from what is no longer usable, and recycle as much of the latter as possible.
- Make a plan with dates and times to repair what you can easily mend.
- For items you can't personally repair, look through your local Yellow Pages and locate the businesses that will fix the items: electrical and appliance repair services, shoe repair persons, seamstresses and tailors, and mechanics. Call or drop by for an estimate.
- If some items prove too costly to fix, see if you can find service organizations like Goodwill or Salvation Army that would be happy to have them as is.

MATERIALS

- Things that need repair; tools; Yellow Pages; phone.

TIME

- An afternoon to round up the items, contact the repair services, and drop them off; more time if you mend the items yourself.

TRASH OR TREASURE?

DONATING OR SELLING USED GOODS

Are your closets and storage areas overflowing with stuff? Your trash can be another's treasure. This Earth Action will help you seize the moment and clean out your home while enabling others to use the items you no longer need.

EARTH ACTION
- Round up any items you are no longer using or were considering discarding.
- Encourage household members to do the same.
- Call around to friends and family and see if they can use some of these items.
- Donate what you or others can't use to a service organization such as Goodwill or the Salvation Army.
- Take your clothing to a second hand store for resale. You will receive a small commission when your clothing sells.
- Consider selling your unwanted items on Ebay or craigslist. Many cities and towns also have shops that will advertise and sell your used items online for a percentage of the selling price.

NOTE: You might also consider having a yard sale.

MATERIALS
- Boxes and bags.

TIME
- One to two hours to round up and sort through your stuff; several hours if you hold a yard sale.

RESOURCE SAVINGS

Every item used by another person lessens the demand for resources to produce a similar item, including packaging and fuel to transport it. You also save resources needed to manage the discarded waste. You're a treasure for the Earth!

2nd Chance Shop

CELEBRATE WITH THE EARTH IN MIND

USING RE-USABLE PARTY PRODUCTS

Birthdays, holidays, and parties can be joyous occasions for the Earth as well, if we use fewer disposable items. The share of waste attributable to paper and plastic plates and cups more than doubled over the past several decades. This Earth Action will help you create a supply of durable, reusable table settings for use at the next large celebration—and all the ones that follow! Enjoy.

RESOURCE SAVINGS

You lessen the demand for the resources and energy necessary to make the disposable tableware and gift wrap, and you save resources needed to manage the waste. That's worth celebrating!

EARTH ACTION

- Identify the kinds of gatherings you host.
- Arrange with a friend or EcoTeam member to borrow the supplies you will need, including: china, glasses, flatware, and fabric tablecloths and napkins.
- If it's not possible to borrow what you need, purchase reusable tableware, such as plastic plates and glasses, that can be washed and used again and again.
- Consider making a joint purchase with a friend so you can share these infrequently-used items.
- Don't forget to save and reuse all gift wrap. Start a new trend: give a gift to a friend in the same paper he or she used to wrap your present.
- Make cloth gift bags or make the wrapping part of the gift. For example, wrap a housewarming gift in a towel or tablecloth.

NOTE: Consider passing this idea along to the person organizing meetings or parties you may attend.

MATERIALS

- A supply of durable, reusable tableware and cloth gift bags.

TIME

- An hour to develop a party supply; time to wash and store it. Add the time required to make cloth gift bags.

Party Dishes

POOP SCOOP

CLEANING UP AFTER YOUR DOG

Poop pollutes. When our pets leave those little surprises, their waste becomes a health risk. When deposited on streets and lawns, it can be washed down storm drains and end up in the watershed. The bacteria, together with other pollutants, can make the water unsafe for swimming and other forms of recreation. The bacteria can also cause health hazards for humans. This Earth Action will show you how to take care of your pet's poop without polluting your neighborhood and its water quality.

EARTH ACTION
- When walking your pet, bring a small trowel or "pooper scooper" and a recycled plastic bag.
- Make sure your pet does not poop or pee directly on the pavement. Choose a grassy or more absorbent area instead. It is less likely the next rainstorm will wash the waste into the storm drains or local tributaries.
- After your pet does it's business, scoop the poop and place it in the bag. Tie it shut until you get home.
- Flush the poop down the toilet so it can be treated in the community sewage or septic system. Your other alternatives are to bury the poop in the ground or place the bag in your garbage can. This does, however, use up valuable landfill space.

MATERIALS
- Trowel or "pooper scooper"; recycled bag or container.

TIME
- A minute or two to scoop and flush.

RESOURCE SAVINGS

You help keep the watershed healthy, protecting fish and wildlife habitats. You also improve the neighborhood for all to enjoy, while giving children a cleaner, healthier place to play.

CUT IT HIGH AND LET IT LIE

MULCHING GRASS

WHY ACT? Your grass clippings can account for as much as 50% of residential yard waste during the peak growing seasons. You can leave these clippings on the lawn to feed the soil. This practice is known as "grasscycling." It enhances the health of your lawn by adding moisture and acting as a natural fertilizer. It also saves you time — no more bagging clippings and dragging them to the curb! This Earth Action will walk you through the "grasscycling" steps.

RESOURCE SAVINGS

By "grasscycling" you save valuable water resources. When using a powered mower, mowing less frequently reduces the amount of harmful emissions entering the atmosphere.

EARTH ACTION

- Mow your lawn to between 2 and 2 1/2 inches to hide clippings.
- Leave the clippings on the lawn. They will break down quickly and not result in thatch.
- Mow the lawn when it's dry to avoid clumping.
- Water deeply, but infrequently. (If you have clay soil it is better to water more frequently, using 1/2 the water each time, for a shorter period of time.)
- If you need a new mower, consider a push mower or an electric mulching lawn mower. The best mulching mowers can blow finely chopped clippings down into your lawn where they disappear from sight, decompose, and fertilize the lawn quickly. An electric mulching mower also cuts down on air pollution.

NOTE: To lessen the burden of maintaining a lawn and the toll it takes on our water supply, consider replacing all or part of your lawn with drought-tolerant plants, herbs and wildflowers, (see "Sustainable Landscaping" on p. 40).

MATERIALS

- Lawn mower; rake (if you are using a push mower) and a yard!

TIME

- "Grasscycling" will substantially reduce the time you are spending on lawn care. Specifics will depend on the size of your lawn.

MULCH! MULCH!

RELATING TO NATURE: ROOTS

PLANTING TREES

 Paper occupies over a third of our landfill space. If you're an average American, you will use seven trees a year to live your life. Why not plant a tree or two to return some of the favor? This Earth Action will help you to appreciate trees so you will be more careful when using products made from them.

EARTH ACTION
- Ask your local government if there is a tree giveaway program in your town or county. If so, get your tree sapling from them. Check out the National Arbor Day Website, www.arborday.org.
- Inquire about local guidelines for planting trees in your neighborhood.
- Purchase a young tree from your local nursery and ask for instructions on how to plant it.
- If you don't have a yard or property of your own, get permission to plant it in a local park or in another place where you can maintain it.
- Take time on a regular basis to care for the tree.

MATERIALS
- One or more saplings and a shovel.

TIME
- Several hours to buy and plant your tree; time to contemplate its wonder.

RESOURCE SAVINGS

If we value the special role trees play in providing the products we require, adding beauty, and supplying the oxygen we need to live, we will be more careful in how we use them. Your caring for the Earth will encourage others to take action!

THANK YOU

FARTHER DOWN THE PATH:

WHY ACT? There is no such thing as garbage in nature, as was stated in the introduction to this section. We human inhabitants of the planet need to learn how to live in harmony with this same law of nature if we aspire to be sustainable for the long run. All the actions in this section are prerequisites to this one. This action will take that effort a quantum leap further—creating and implementing a plan to achieve a zero-garbage household.

EARTH ACTION

- The starting point for taking this journey is creating a healthy attitude. The attitude we recommend is to see yourself as walking a sustainability path rather than fixating on avoiding garbage.
- If you live with others, you will need to have their participation. Call a meeting and explain why you wish to do this and ask for their cooperation.
- The essence of this path is that everything brought into your house has to meet two criteria: it's able to be recycled or reused or it isn't brought home. Success is quite measurable—no garbage services are needed anymore—your household waste stream is zero!
- Empty onto your kitchen floor what you are currently sending to the waste stream. If you are taking the previous actions of this section, what is lying in front of you is the stuff not taken by your local recycling center or what is not compostable.
- Write down your plan to reuse, recycle or find alternative products that allow you to avoid purchasing each of these items in the future. Add to this list items that might be in your waste stream at other times of the year. Also consider items that are durable but not permanent, like toothbrushes. Make sure the plan has a time frame by when you will eliminate each item on your list.
- Suggestions for accomplishing your plan:
  - Call your local recycling agency. Ask if there is anyplace where these materials can be recycled. If it's possible to do so, but the location isn't convenient, you might ask your neighborhood EcoTeam to share the responsibility.
  - Get creative on re-use. Perhaps there is someone in your life who could use these materials in their work or hobby. Call and ask them. Perhaps there is a place in your home, such as a workshop space, where re-use and restoration projects can be kept and worked on. An excellent source for reuse ideas is the book *Choose to Reuse* by Nikki and David Goldbeck.
  - For items that you can't recycle or re-use, find an alternative that is recyclable or change your purchasing habits.

SPECIAL NOTE:

Each action you take through this program is a sustainable lifestyle practice to enable you to better steward our natural resources. These actions are doable and common sense—the challenge for most of us is taking the time to translate our good intention into action, and being consistent. Some EcoTeam participants have desired to go farther, and have asked us what the frontier of environmentally sustainable living looks like. This action and the others at the end of each section represent the path ahead. To take them will require an inventive and deliberate approach because our society does not yet have the mechanisms in place to easily support these choices. These actions, therefore, are for those with a pioneering spirit and a willingness to help blaze the trail.

ACTION continued on next page

A ZERO GARBAGE HOUSEHOLD

- Following are some examples of the kinds of garbage you are likely to find and some creative ideas for what you might do. Use these ideas as illustrations of how you might think about the issue, rather than an exhaustive list. *Plastic packaging*—Use as wall or ceiling insulation, or replace this product with one that has recyclable packaging or no packaging. Ask the store to take back the packaging. *Bottle caps*—Fill a big jar and use as a doorstop, scout for a classroom teacher that might be able to use them for art projects, drink filtered tap water, keep reusing the bottle for other purposes. *Yogurt containers*—Buy big tubs and re-use or make your own yogurt. This raises your awareness about future purchasing decisions.

• Once you have started eliminating these kinds of things from your waste stream, the real work will be the vigilance of sustaining this action as a long-term sustainable lifestyle practice. It will be challenging no doubt, but rewarding for you and the Earth.

NOTE: Translate as much of this learning as possible while you are traveling, moving about your community and at work. While you may not have the same freedom of choice, much is possible to lower your overall waste stream if you plan for it in advance. And who knows what may happen with a choice comment to those people whom you wish to encourage to reduce their waste stream. Most people want to be better stewards of resources, they just need some friendly encouragement.

MATERIALS
• Pen, paper, household members, adventuresome spirit, and lots of ingenuity.

TIME
• Two to three hours for your household to evaluate your current and future waste stream and create a plan to eliminate it. A few moments to examine each product you buy or bring into your house to make sure you can recycle or reuse it.

RESOURCE SAVINGS
• All the resources not needed to produce and ship the products or packaging you are eliminating from your waste stream. All the resources not needed to landfill or incinerate these materials.

ACTION NOTES

WASTING WATER IS ALL WET— ACTION LOG

Actions	Action Plan		Discussed with Household	Action Done	Points
AquaCop	Day:	Time:	☐	☐	2
Tanks A Lot	Day:	Time:	☐	☐	2
Go With the Flow	Day:	Time:	☐	☐	3
AquaTech	Day:	Time:	☐	☐	3
Am I Clean Yet?	Day:	Time:	☐	☐	3
Scrub-A-Dub Rub	Day:	Time:	☐	☐	2
Scrub-A-Dub Tub	Day:	Time:	☐	☐	2
All Bottled Up	Day:	Time:	☐	☐	1
Hold the Salt	Day:	Time:	☐	☐	4
Pure and Simple	Day:	Time:	☐	☐	1
No-Phos-For-Us	Day:	Time:	☐	☐	4
A No-Rainer	Day:	Time:	☐	☐	4
The Lawn Ranger	Day:	Time:	☐	☐	3
A Natural Lawn	Day:	Time:	☐	☐	4
A Master Waterer	Day:	Time:	☐	☐	3
Down By The River	Day:	Time:	☐	☐	4
Relating to Nature: Where My Water Comes From	Day:	Time:	☐	☐	1
Farther Down the Path: Sustainable Landscaping	Day:	Time:	☐	☐	6

STEP 2 WASTING WATER IS ALL WET

WATER EFFICIENCY

WATER AND YOU

Water is the substance of life on this planet; 80% of the Earth's surface is water, and less than 1% is available and potable. It is 70% of our body weight. It is the principle substance that runs through our veins. It is one of the primary things we bequeath to our children to enable them to live. To be stewards of this precious resource requires that we use it carefully. Unfortunately, we are not doing this. Our wasteful practices and the pollution of our groundwater are deteriorating the available supplies.

Even in places where the water supply still seems adequate, extensive water use causes environmental problems. Great amounts of energy are used to transport, heat, and treat water, using up our fossil fuels and contributing to air pollution and global warming. Water from underground aquifers is often being used faster than it is replenished. Not only will the aquifers run out at some point, but cave-ins in the emptying aquifers damage them in ways that cannot be repaired.

At a personal level, reducing water use will lower your water and sewer bills, or if you have a well, it will lower your utility bills, since electricity is required to pump and heat the water. Stewarding our precious and finite supply of water is an essential part of living an environmentally sustainable lifestyle. In this section you will learn how to implement the lifestyle practices needed to be a responsible steward of the elixir of life.

AQUACOP

FINDING WATER LEAKS IN YOUR HOME

 A small drip from a leaky faucet isn't a drop in the bucket. A slow leak can waste over 10 gallons of water a day. Add up the water loss from every possible leak in your plumbing, and that's a huge amount of wasted water. An EPA study found that a single family home leaks 9.5 gallons per person per day (on average). This Earth Action will help you plug your leaks. It will be time well spent.

EARTH ACTION

- Scout out leaks under sinks and around showers, tubs, and toilets, and make a list. Look for puddles, drips, water stains, and mildew. Listen for toilet tanks that continue to run. Toilet leaks can be silent. To sleuth out a toilet leak, add food coloring to the tank (not the bowl). Don't flush. Instead, check in half an hour to see if any of the dye seeped into the toilet bowl. If it did, you have a leak.
- If you have a water meter, check to see if it moves while water is not being used. If it does, there is a leak.
- Call a plumber to fix any leaks, or develop a schedule for repairing them yourself.

NOTE: Remember to recheck on a regular basis.

MATERIALS

- Paper and pencil; food coloring; name and number of plumber; materials to fix leaks you want to repair.

TIME

- About 15 minutes to check for leaks and call a plumber, more if you fix the leaks yourself.

RESOURCE SAVINGS

The more leaks you find, the more water you save. In one day, a steady drip from your faucet can waste 40 gallons of water and a leaking toilet can waste as much as 200 gallons. Your detective skills are helping preserve your community's water supply.

TANKS A LOT
REDUCING WATER USED FOR TOILET FLUSHING

WHY ACT? The average tank on the back of your toilet holds about 3.5 gallons of water. Only 1.6 gallons are needed per flush, but all 3.5 go down the drain. This easy Earth Action will help you reduce the amount of water that fills the tank so that less is used each time you flush.

OK, A LITTLE TO THE LEFT!

RESOURCE SAVINGS

A commercial dam will save you up to one gallon per flush, or about 2,000 gallons a year. A homemade dam will save 3/4 gallon per flush, or about 1500 gallons per year. These savings are just for one person. They will increase substantially based on the number of individuals in your household. For a small effort, you made a big contribution!

EARTH ACTION
- Purchase a toilet dam for each toilet in your house from a home supply store or on-line. They should cost under $10 apiece and save 40% of the water per flush.
- Install the dam(s).
- If you cannot get a commercial toilet dam, or don't wish to spend the money, make your own for free. While this homemade approach displaces only about 20% of the water per flush, it has an impact. Here's how to make a dam:
  - Clean an empty half-gallon plastic jug. Soak the jug to remove labels.
  - Fill the jug about half full with wet sand or gravel. Secure the lid tightly.
  - Put the jug in the corner of the tank, making sure it does not interfere with any moving parts.
  - Repeat these steps for each toilet in your home.

NOTE: You may want to go even further and consider replacing your toilet with a low-flow model. Some now require as little as 1.6 gallons per flush. See if your municipality offers rebates and congratulate yourself for taking the plunge.

MATERIALS
- Commercial toilet dam(s), or half-gallon jug(s) and lid(s), sand or gravel, or low-flow toilet(s).

TIME
- Half an hour to purchase or assemble a dam or jug; a couple of minutes to install each one; longer to install a toilet.

GO WITH THE FLOW
REDUCING THE NUMBER OF TOILET FLUSHES

 Almost 30% of the water that comes into your home goes down the toilet. Every time you flush the average toilet, you use about 3.5 gallons of water. Even if you have a low-flow toilet, you still probably flush several times a day. Each flush uses your supply of fresh water, the same supply you need for other purposes, such as drinking, showering, laundering, and cleaning.

EARTH ACTION
• Here's the rule: "If it's yellow, let it mellow. If it's brown, flush it down."
• Get members of your household together. Discuss this action and decide how many "pees in a pot" you want before flushing.

MATERIALS
• None. But you may need to use some creative persuasion skills on your household and uninitiated friends.

TIME
• 10 minutes to meet with household members.

RESOURCE SAVINGS

If you have a standard toilet, you save approximately 3.5 gallons every time you don't flush. If a household of 4 reduces its daily flushes from 20 to 10 or less, (at 3.5 gallons per flush) that would save about 35 gallons a day, or 12,500 gallons of water a year. That's enough to fill a small-sized swimming pool.

WOW!

HEY! LET IT MELLOW!

AQUATECH
INSTALLING WATER-SAVING DEVICES

WHY ACT? Did you know that showers and faucets account for approximately 30% of your indoor water use? Installing water-saving devices on showers and faucets is an easy and inexpensive way to substantially reduce your water use. Most of these devices have an on-off switch that allows additional savings. And, since showers are more than 50% hot water, you will save on energy as well. For a small initial investment, this Earth Action will yield a regular water-savings dividend for you and everyone else who shares your water supply.

RESOURCE SAVINGS

You can save up to 60% of the water you use while showering and about 50% of the water you use at the sink. If you use the showerhead's on-off control, you will save even more. What an effervescent action!

EARTH ACTION
- Check to see if your local utility company offers free energy audits that may include low-flow showerheads and faucet aerators for sinks. If so, schedule an audit.
- If not, purchase from a home supply store or on-line.
- Replace your showerheads and attach the aerators to your faucets.

MATERIALS
- Phone book and phone, low-flow showerheads and faucet aerators, preferably with on-off controls.

TIME
- A few minutes to call the utility company and some time for the audit; or 30 minutes to purchase the items and a few minutes to install them; no extra time to use them.

THANK YOU, I'VE ALWAYS WANTED ONE OF THOSE!

3

AM I CLEAN YET?

REDUCING THE USE OF SHOWER AND BATH WATER

 How much water do you need to get your body clean? The average shower uses five gallons per minute. This means you could save 25 gallons of water just by staying in the shower for five minutes instead of ten. By switching to a low-flow showerhead, you could save even more (see "AquaTech" p. 26). A bath can use 30 to 60 gallons of water—over twice the amount you need for a five-minute shower. This Earth Action will help you reduce your personal water use without sacrificing the pleasure of a warm shower. Now you have something to sing about as you lather up!

EARTH ACTION

- Time your average shower to become aware of your personal water use, and record the number of minutes it takes on your Sustainable Lifestyle Assessment.
- Determine how much time you actually need by taking your shower in a purposeful manner. Continue to time your shower for a few days until you get into the new habit.
- A good goal to strive for is five minutes or under. To achieve this— or a time that better suits you—you can either take shorter showers or turn off the water while you are soaping up.
- Catch warm-up water for your shower in a bucket or pan, and use to water plants or flush the toilet.

MATERIALS

- A watch or clock, paper and pen.

TIME

- Here's one where you end up with more time.

RESOURCE SAVINGS

You save five gallons for every minute less you shower or run the water, as well as energy to heat that water and electricity to pump it to you. Now you're clean and green!

SCRUB-A-DUB RUB

REDUCING WATER USED IN PERSONAL CARE

WHY ACT? Does the water run while you wash your face, brush your teeth, or shave? Letting the faucet run just while you brush your teeth—for three minutes in the morning and three minutes at night—uses up to nine gallons of water per day. You can easily use another eight gallons if you shave with the tap on. This simple Earth Action will help you reduce your personal water use at the sink by as much as 70%.

RESOURCE SAVINGS

Making this action a habit saves about 7 gallons of water each day. That's over 2,500 gallons of water every year or the amount of water needed for a five-minute shower every day for over three months! Your awareness goes a long way!

EARTH ACTION
- To wash hands and face: Run the water at low force to wet your skin and the soap; then turn it off. Wash. Turn the water back on to rinse off.
- To brush your teeth: Run the water at low force to wet your toothbrush and fill a glass with a little water for rinsing; turn the faucet off. Brush your teeth and rinse. Turn the water on briefly to rinse your brush and glass.
- To shave: Run the water at low force to wet your face and clean and rinse the razor while shaving. Turn off the water when not needed.

MATERIALS
- A glass for rinsing.

TIME
- No additional time.

EVERY DROP COUNTS

USE WITH CARE

SCRUB-A-DUB TUB

REDUCING WATER USED TO WASH DISHES

Washing dishes by hand while the water is running for just 10 minutes uses about 15 gallons of water, much of it wasted. This method wastes water even if you turn off the tap while you scrub. Washing a small load in a dishwasher uses up to 12 gallons of water. There is a water-efficient way to wash your dishes, however. This Earth Action will help to reduce the water you use and impress all with your dishwashing skill.

EARTH ACTION
• Wash dishes in a tub or partitioned sink. Here's how:
  - Fill the tub or section of the sink with hot, soapy water. Use biodegradable liquid soap. Put dishes in and let them soak well.
  - Scrub dishes.
  - Fill a second tub, or the other half of the sink, about two-thirds full with hot water.
  - Dunk and swish dishes in the rinse water to remove soapy film.
• Only run the dishwasher when you have a full load.

MATERIALS
• Two tubs or a partitioned sink; biodegradable dishwashing liquid.

TIME
• About 5-10 minutes per meal to wash dishes.

RESOURCE SAVINGS

Each time you wash your dishes by hand efficiently, you use about eight gallons of water instead of up to 12. You could save four gallons each day, or almost 1,500 gallons in one year—enough water for six months worth of dishwashing. That's a sparkling performance!

ALL BOTTLED UP

DRINKING REFRIGERATED WATER

WHY ACT? How much water goes down the drain before you get water cold enough to drink? One cup? Two cups? Six? On average, 24 cups of clean water are wasted each time we wait for the water to turn cold by letting it run for one minute. If you live in a city or the suburbs, this lost freshwater will actually have to travel through a sewage treatment plant. That's not only wasted water but wasted energy to treat the water. This Earth Action will help you reduce to zero the amount of water you let slip down the drain just to get a cold drink!

RESOURCE SAVINGS

If you've been letting the water run like this once a day, you'll now save about 550 gallons of water per person in your home each year. That's enough water for about 14 baths! You've helped preserve a precious resource for us all.

EARTH ACTION
• Fill a reusable bottle or container with tap water and keep it in the refrigerator. Now you have cold, refreshing drinking water on hand at all times.

MATERIALS
• Reusable bottle or container.

TIME
• About 1 minute to fill the container.

HOLD THE SALT

MINIMIZING SALT USED BY WATER SOFTENERS

Water softeners use common table salt (sodium chloride) to soften the water you use at home. Because of this process, the softened water that is discharged into the sewer system has a high level of dissolved salts. Municipal wastewater treatment plants cannot remove these salts, which can be toxic to certain aquatic animals. By reducing the amount of salt you use in the water softening process and/or by reducing the amount of soft water used in your home, you will reduce chloride (salt) toxicity in local lakes, streams and rivers.

RESOURCE SAVINGS

A family of four with a 25% annual reduction in salt usage would save about 150 pounds of salt and 3,000 gallons of water (that would otherwise be used in the softening process.) You'll also help improve the quality of our local water supply—for aquatic life and for humans!

EARTH ACTION
- Get a water softener "tune-up."
  - Have a local supplier inspect your water softener to adjust the settings for the most efficient salt usage.
  - Ask him/her to help you determine if you are using soft water only where necessary. Water used for washing (dishes and clothes) and for baths and showers needs to be softened. Outdoor faucets, toilets and cold water taps should not use softened water. If you need to replumb, call a plumber for the most cost-effective method.
  - If you find that your water softener needs to be replaced, make sure to buy a metered demand type with a high-efficiency resin.
- If you want to go further:
  - For softener systems triggered by a timer, try increasing the setting by one day. If you don't notice any hardness effects (poor lathering of soaps or shampoos) after two regeneration cycles, increase the setting by another day.
  - For softener systems triggered by a built-in meter, increase the setting by 100 gallons and watch for hardness effects. If you don't notice any effects after two weeks, increase the setting another 100 gallons.
  - Repeat these adjustments until you notice hardness effects, then back off the settings accordingly.

MATERIALS
- Water softener owner's manual, telephone, and telephone directory.

TIME
- Half an hour to review your owner's manual; a few minutes to adjust the settings. Several hours if you decide to redo plumbing.

PURE AND SIMPLE

CHECKING WATER PURITY

WHY ACT? We've come to take our drinking water for granted, but just how pure is it? If you're pumping water from your own well, you may wish to check the quality because individual wells are not regulated. If you are on a municipal system, your water is probably fine, but you may want to test it anyway just to satisfy yourself. This simple Earth Action will help you make sure the water from your faucet is pure.

RESOURCE SAVINGS

By ensuring the water in your home is pure, you save the most important resource of all: your health and that of other household members. You also save having to drink bottled water and lessen the demand for resources used to extract, package, and transport the water.

EARTH ACTION

- Identify your water source. Are you on a municipal supply, or does your water come from a well on your property?
- Call your county health department or municipal water authority for information on the water quality in your area and, if you decide to test your water, ask them to recommend a certified laboratory.
- Contact the lab and arrange to have your water tested.
- If your water is contaminated, ask your local health department for advice.
- Remedy the problem. If you decide you need a water filtration system, research and install it.

MATERIALS

- Phone book and phone.

TIME

- Half an hour to find a lab and collect the sample; some time to deliver it for testing. Half an hour to call your water supplier for water quality information

NO PHOS-FOR-US

EARTH-FRIENDLY CAR WASHING

How and where you wash your car or truck makes a difference to our local environment! The soap, together with dirt and oil washed from your vehicle, can find its way into local streams, wells and groundwater through storm drains which are not linked to a water treatment plant. This pollution harms water quality and aquatic life. This Earth Action will help you keep your vehicle and your waters clean.

EARTH ACTION

- Wash your vehicle on grass or gravel instead of the street or driveway to help filter the soapy water and grime.
- Use soap which is biodegradable. To better conserve water, make sure your hose has an on-off switch or nozzle.
- If you use a bucket of soap and water, pour what is left in your bucket down the sink so it can be treated.
- To have the least environmental impact, go to a car wash that treats and recycles the wash water. Most car washes do this; check with them to confirm. If you take your car to be washed at a charity event, make sure they have a storm drain catchment kit to trap oil and other harmful chemicals.

MATERIALS

- Hose, nozzle, bucket, sponges or rags, biodegradable soap, a lawn or a gravel area to park on, commercial car wash.

TIME

- No extra time required.

RESOURCE SAVINGS

Your efforts will *protect* aquatic habitats and water quality.

A NO RAINER

REDUCING THE AMOUNT OF WATER GOING INTO THE SEWER SYSTEM

 WHY ACT? Sanitary sewers are designed to transport wastes during peak use periods but are not designed to transport the large volume of clear water that results from rainstorms or snow-melt. Improperly installed roof drain systems can allow this clear water to drain into your basement, and from there into your local sewer. When your local sanitary sewer system is overloaded by too much clear water, it can back-up in basements and overflow manholes. Both of these situations create public health and environmental hazards. It is important to direct water from your roof drain system away from the house. This Earth Action will help you avoid taxing the local sewer system and will help keep your basement dry.

RESOURCE SAVINGS

The environmental and public health benefits from avoiding sewer system back-ups are priceless. And you'll help your local wastewater treatment plant save the costs of handling excess water in the sewer system.

EARTH ACTION

- Check the gutters and roof drains and remove any leaves or other debris that may block water flow. If leaf accumulation is a recurring problem, consider installing commercial gutter shields.
- If your roof drain downspouts discharge too close to the house, install extensions that carry the water at least six feet away from the foundation. Use additional pieces of downspout or open gutters for the extensions. Place a splash block at the end of the extension to spread out the water as it runs onto your lawn, or collect the water in a rain barrel. This reduces the potential for soil erosion. (Check out "roll-up" extensions.)

NOTE: If the sump pump in your basement discharges into the sanitary sewer system, be aware that this is not a legal hookup. Contact an expert to change your connections so that the sump pump discharges groundwater into a surface or subsurface drainage system. Your local water department has a guide if you want to do this work yourself.

MATERIALS

- Ladder and gloves to inspect and clean gutters, eye protection, gutter covers with hardware, hand tools, ladder, downspout pipe with hardware, splash blocks.

TIME

- One hour to inspect the rain gutters and one to four more hours to clean the gutters if necessary. A few more hours to install gutter shields and/or extensions.

THE LAWN RANGER
REDUCING WATER USED FOR LAWNS

 If you have a lawn and water it, there's a good chance it's being overwatered by a third. The average quarter-acre of lawn gets about 22,000 gallons of water a week more than it needs! This Earth Action will show you how the grass can be greener on your property. This is one of the most important water-saving efforts you can make.

EARTH ACTION

- Most established lawns need only one inch of water a week. To give your lawn the inch it needs:
  - Place three cans at various spots in one area of your lawn. Turn on the sprinkler and time how long it takes for one inch of water to accumulate in each can.
  - Add the three times together, divide by three and that's how long you'll need to water that area.
  - Each time you move your sprinkler, water for the same amount of time.
- To retain the water you use:
  - Water early in the morning or early in the evening to avoid evaporation that occurs during the heat of the day.
  - Keep your grass between 2" and 3" tall to provide natural shade that will help the soil stay moist. Leave grass clippings on the lawn to retain moisture.

MATERIALS
- Three cans, sprinkler, watch.

TIME
- A few minutes to calculate the amount of time you need to water; lots of time freed up by this new watering technique.

RESOURCE SAVINGS

You can save at least one-third of the water you now use by making sure your lawn only gets the inch of water it needs each week. Your water-saving habits are an important contribution to your community and planet.

HEY, LOOK AT ME! I'VE GOT AN INCH!

A NATURAL LAWN

REDUCING THE USE OF WEED KILLERS AND FERTILIZERS

WHY ACT? If you have a lawn, you may be using weed killers and fertilizers to keep it green and weed-free. Unfortunately, toxic chemicals in weed killers and fertilizers often wash off your lawn into local streams and ground water, eventually polluting the watershed and tributaries. This Earth Action will show you how to create a natural lawn and help protect the health of your family, wildlife, and our local resources.

RESOURCE SAVINGS

By "greening" your lawn, you prevent the pollution from weed killers and fertilizers from flowing into the water systems while making your lawn a natural place for you, your family and neighbors to enjoy.

EARTH ACTION

• If you fertilize at all, use organic compost instead of chemical fertilizers. Fertilizers can act as pollutants once they enter our waterways. You can either create your own compost, or purchase it from a garden supply center.

• Accept a few weeds, like clover, which can coexist nicely with your lawn. Hand pull the ugly ones before they seed, and leave the others alone.

• Overseed thin areas in the spring and fall to crowd out weeds. Just rake to expose the soil, spread the seed, and cover with 1/4 inch of compost or soil.

NOTE: To lessen the burden of maintaining a lawn and the toll it takes on the water supply and the pollutants going into the watershed, consider replacing all or part of your lawn with drought-tolerant plants, herbs and wildflowers. (See Sustainable Landscaping, p.40).

MATERIALS

• Natural compost, soil, seeds, rake and weed pulling tools.

TIME

• A couple of hours to pull weeds and fertilize with compost.

A MASTER WATERER

REDUCING WATER USED FOR GARDENING

 If you have a garden, at least 50% of the water you use may be wasted through inefficiency. You probably use about 60 gallons of water every time you water for just 10 minutes. This Earth Action will show you how to be a master waterer in your own little corner of paradise.

EARTH ACTION

- Check all hose connections to make sure there are no leaks, and install hose washers where needed.
- Make sure your hose nozzle has an on-off switch (like a trigger mechanism).
- Water early in the morning or early evening to avoid evaporation that occurs during the heat of the day. Direct the water to the soil where it is needed. A deep soaking once a week is more effective than shallow watering every day.
- Cover your garden with a protective blanket of organic mulch, such as wood chips, to retain moisture.
- Whenever possible, landscape with native plants that require little water and upkeep.

NOTE: To minimize your water use even more, you may want to consider using grey water or installing a drip irrigation system, which can save up to 50% of the water used with conventional methods. Ask your local nursery for details.

MATERIALS

- Hose washers, on-off switch, mulch, native plants.

TIME

- A few minutes to check for leaks and install washers; half an hour or more to add mulch, depending on the size of your garden; more time if you install a drip irrigation system; no extra time to set out native plants instead of others.

RESOURCE SAVINGS

By watering your garden more efficiently, you can save up to 50% of the water you normally use. You've earned a master waterer degree. Congratulations!

DOWN BY THE RIVER

CREATING A SUSTAINABLE STREAMSIDE ECOSYSTEM

If you live near a stream, the health of your streamside ecosystem is in jeopardy if you have invasive, non-native plants or monoculture vegetation, both of which contribute to soil erosion and stream pollution. To create a sustainable streamside ecosystem you need to have diverse, native and multi-storied vegetation. Native plants need little or no watering. By "going native", you'll also reduce the need for pollutants such as fertilizers, pesticides and herbicides. This Earth Action will help you protect your property, and will support and protect fish and wildlife habitat. You and other residents will enjoy the benefits of clean water and recreational opportunities.

RESOURCE SAVINGS

You will contribute to fish spawning habitat by reducing clouded streams caused by erosion. Hardy, streamside, native vegetation also helps filter out pollutants that may have otherwise entered the stream. You will also contribute to the preservation of your own property by stemming streamside erosion.

EARTH ACTION
- If you have invasive non-native vegetation or monoculture vegetation (a single type of plant), revegetate with native, ecologically diverse plants of varying heights.
- If your streambank has begun to erode, seek expert help to repair it.

MATERIALS
- Garden tools and gloves, native plants, phone and directory for nurseries and expertise.

TIME
- A few hours to several days depending on the extent of the problem.

RELATING TO NATURE: WHERE MY WATER COMES FROM

GET ACQUAINTED WITH YOUR WATERSHED

The water you use to drink, wash, and cook comes from a watershed near your home. Every community, whether it is mountainous or flat, urban or rural, is part of a watershed. Within each watershed, all water drains to the lowest point, carrying with it soil particles, oil, road salt, organic materials, pesticides, and fertilizers. This Earth Action will help you identify your local watershed so you will become more aware of what you can do to keep it healthy.

EARTH ACTION

- Contact your local, county or state environmental conservation agency (listed in the Yellow Pages) and ask for information about your local watershed, including where the water comes from and what, if anything, is being done to protect the quality and supply.
- Contribute to keeping your watershed healthy by not pouring toxic products down the drain or outside your house. (See Toxic Sleuth, p.85)
- For valuable water information check the EPA Website: www.epa.gov/safewater.

MATERIALS

- Phone book and phone.

TIME

- 15 minutes to make the phone call, or check the website.

RESOURCE SAVINGS

Knowing about your watershed provides you with the motivation to protect this precious resource so essential to your life. Your gentle way of treating the Earth will touch a lot of people.

LOCAL WATER TABLE

WELL

WELL

LOCAL WATER SUPPLY

USE ME WITH CARE SO THAT YOU AND OTHERS CAN HAVE WATER IN THE FUTURE.

FARTHER DOWN THE PATH:

WHY ACT? The actions listed in this section will help you develop water-efficient lifestyle practices. There is one area of water use, however, which has significant environmental consequences and deserves more attention. If you have a typical lawn there's a good chance that half of your household's yearly water use goes into maintaining it. If you live in a community where your water is supplied by a municipal water utility, summer peak use times often require a substantial amount of water be on reserve for watering lawns. This in turn requires that municipalities go to great lengths to have this water available. They often have to build special wells, set up mechanisms to transport water over great distances, support the development of new reservoirs and other activities that have major environmental impacts. This action can help you reduce your water use by up to 50% while creating a self-sustaining natural landscape that is highly attractive and low maintenance.

RESOURCE SAVINGS

You will reduce up to 50% of your yearly water use, lessen your environmental impact on regional water resources and wildlife habitats, and eliminate the need for fertilizers for keeping up a green lawn. All the free time gained by not having to mow or maintain your lawn is yours to spend frivolously.

ACTION continued on next page

SUSTAINABLE LANDSCAPING

EARTH ACTION

- Develop a plan for creating a natural landscape, often called xeriscaping. It's done by planting native, hybrid and adapted plants that can survive well on the normal rainfall of your region. A water-saving landscape can be beautiful and highly distinctive. It also provides habitat to local wildlife.
- In creating your plan, seek professional advice from a landscape designer or your local nursery. Your goal is to reduce the percentage of lawn in your yard. When purchasing plants from nurseries, let them know you wish to see them stock more native plants. This will help build demand for an increased variety of native plants in your area, which will help provide impetus to others wishing to develop sustainable landscapes.
- Depending on your budget, time, and aesthetic preference, phase in your plan.

NOTE: If you wish to maintain a flower garden, consider planting more perennials which once established require little supplemental water and maintenance. If you desire to have some grass areas, consider planting ornamental drought-tolerant varieties. They are attractive, and provide a natural grassland look with no watering or maintenance. If you are not completely xeriscaping your lawn or garden, and while establishing your natural landscape, remember to use the water-efficient practices described earlier in this section.

MATERIALS

- Pen and paper to create your plan, native plants, garden tools, advice of landscape designer or nursery, or the book *Xeriscape Gardening*, by Connie Ellefson, MacMillan publishing.

TIME

- Several hours to consult a landscape designer or nursery. Considerable time and pleasure if you create your sustainable landscape yourself.

ACTION NOTES

GETTING A CHARGE OUT OF
SAVING ENERGY—ACTION LOG

Actions	Action Plan		Discussed with Household	Action Done	Points
A Bright Idea	Day:	Time:	☐	☐	1
Plug Your Electricity Leaks	Day:	Time:	☐	☐	2
How Green Is Your Computer?	Day:	Time:	☐	☐	2
Light of Your Life	Day:	Time:	☐	☐	4
Wear It Again Sam	Day:	Time:	☐	☐	2
Meet Your Water Heater	Day:	Time:	☐	☐	2
Fridge Physical	Day:	Time:	☐	☐	1
Better A Sweater	Day:	Time:	☐	☐	3
Furnace Fling	Day:	Time:	☐	☐	3
Putting On Airs	Day:	Time:	☐	☐	3
Chill Out	Day:	Time:	☐	☐	3
Chill In	Day:	Time:	☐	☐	2
Fans Are Cool	Day:	Time:	☐	☐	2
What You See Is What You Breathe	Day:	Time:	☐	☐	3
Relating to Nature: An Enlightening Experience	Day:	Time:	☐	☐	1
Farther Down the Path: A Sustainable Energy Household	Day:	Time:	☐	☐	6

STEP 3

GETTING A CHARGE OUT OF SAVING ENERGY

ENERGY EFFICIENCY

ENERGY AND YOU

As Americans, we use a significant percentage of the planet's supply of fossil fuels —petroleum, natural gas, and coal— to provide energy to our homes. In one year, an American uses as much of these fossil fuels as someone in a developing country uses for his or her entire life. The burning of these fuels causes air pollution and contributes to global warming and acid rain. Global warming is the most daunting threat facing our planet and future generations. For both environmental and moral reasons, we must learn to more efficiently use our precious energy resources.

How are we doing in stewarding our energy resources? Unfortunately, not very well. As Americans, we waste as much as 75% of the energy we use through inefficiency or lack of awareness.

Fortunately, there is much we can do through energy efficiency to get more comfort and benefit from our energy use while using less — often considerably less. Since saving energy means reducing our impact on global warming and saving money, being a responsible steward of our energy resources is not only the right thing to do, it's intelligent! In this section of your journey, you will take action to implement the sustainable lifestyle practices needed to steward our precious energy resources.

A BRIGHT IDEA
USING ELECTRICITY MORE EFFICIENTLY

 You can be a global citizen every time you leave the room. All you need to do is turn things off. This Earth Action will help you remember to go through life with the Earth in mind—and lower your electric bill at the same time.

EARTH ACTION
- This Earth Action is about remembering to turn things off. Here's how:
  - If you are the last one out of the room, turn the lights off. It requires less energy to turn a light back on than to leave it on in the first place. This applies to fluorescents, too.
  - When you leave a room, turn off the radio, CD player, TV, and DVD player.
- If you forget to turn the lights off regularly, consider installing motion sensors to turn lights on only when someone is in the room. You might also use light timers (available at most hardware stores) to turn lights off and on when you are away from home for an extended period of time, instead of just leaving the lights on.

MATERIALS
- Timers and your new awareness.

TIME
- A couple of extra seconds.

RESOURCE SAVINGS

You save energy and money and, if your utility company uses fossil fuels to generate electricity, you improve air quality and reduce global warming. Now that's powerful!

PLUG YOUR ELECTRICITY LEAKS
TURNING OFF APPLIANCES—ALL THE WAY

WHY ACT? American TVs consume the output of 21 large power plants. It takes one large power plant to supply power for all these TV sets shut-off! Many other types of home appliances use electricity even when turned off. In an average home, the common mix of televisions, CD and DVD players, and other appliances use about 50 watts of electricity 24 hours per day. Over a year, that equals 438 kilowatt hours and costs about $33. This Earth Action will show you how to cut down on wasted electricity and reduce pollution (through burning less fossil fuels to produce electricity).

RESOURCE SAVINGS

You save energy and money and reduce global warming.

EARTH ACTION
- The simplest way to stop energy leaks is to plug the appliances that leak the most electricity—such as televisions—into a switched cord or power strip. That way you can easily turn off the power to these appliances when not in use.
- If possible, unplug any devices and chargers that have a block-shaped transformer on the plug when they are not in use (or turn off with a power strip).
- When you buy new equipment, look for the EnergyStar® label. Appliances that meet new EnergyStar® guidelines use much less standby power. For more information, check the Energy Star® website at: www.energystar.gov.

MATERIALS
- Extension cord or power strip with an on-off switch.

TIME
- A few seconds every day; 30 minutes to check the website.

HOW GREEN IS YOUR COMPUTER?

ENERGY EFFICIENT COMPUTER USE

One of the fastest growing uses of electricity in homes today is computer equipment. The electricity used by a computer and printer left on 24 hours a day results in more than a ton of carbon dioxide in the atmosphere and costs about $115 per year. This Earth Action will show you how to reduce energy use, cut pollution and save money on your utility bills.

EARTH ACTION

- When purchasing, make sure your new computer, printer or fax machine has the EnergyStar® label. EnergyStar® equipment can be set to save energy by powering down in a "sleep" mode when not in use.
- Make sure your EnergyStar® computer equipment has the "sleep" feature enabled. You'll cut the energy use by half during the periods when your system is powered down. Set it to "sleep" when not in use for more than 10 or 15 minutes.
- Shut off your computer equipment when not in use for two hours or more. Unlike the earliest personal computers and hard drives, modern computers are designed for tens of thousands of on-off cycles.

MATERIALS

- Your existing or new equipment, and maybe your operating system manual or "Help" files.

TIME

- A few minutes.

RESOURCE SAVINGS

You save energy and money and reduce pollution and global warming from burning fossil fuels.

LIGHT OF YOUR LIFE
INSTALLING ENERGY EFFICIENT LIGHTING

There's a new way to light up your life: light bulbs! But not the ones you're familiar with. The incandescent light bulb most of us use has been surpassed by the more efficient compact fluorescent. It screws into regular incandescent bulb sockets and uses about 70% less electricity to provide the same amount of light as a standard bulb. While compact fluorescents are more expensive than incandescents, they will last about 10,000 hours compared with 1,000 for the typical incandescent bulb. This means they will last for about eight years, but you will get your investment back and start saving money in less than half that time. And the savings continue throughout the second half of the bulb's life! This Earth Action is dedicated to saving you money and reducing pollution for the planet.

RESOURCE SAVINGS

Saving electricity reduces pollution and global warming caused by the fossil fuels most power plants burn to provide your electricity. One compact fluorescent saves the equivalent of about 600 pounds of coal over the life of the bulb. What a bright idea!

HOW MANY PEOPLE DOES IT TAKE TO SCREW IN A COMPACT FLUORESCENT BULB?

ONE INDIVIDUAL WHO CARES ABOUT THE EARTH!

EARTH ACTION
- Do a room-by-room inventory of all your lighting fixtures that are on at least two hours a day, the number of bulbs they require, and their wattages. As you do this inventory, look for opportunities to use only the lighting required for the task.
- Purchase from a home supply store or on line.
- To determine which compact fluorescents to purchase, remember:
  - Compact fluorescents come in different sizes but are generally slightly larger than the standard bulb with equivalent wattage.
  - The color spectrum of bulbs varies from one manufacturer to another.
  - Some compact fluorescents can be used with a dimmer switch.
- Call your local electric utility company to find out if it includes free compact fluorescents with a home energy audit or offers rebates.
- Put together a plan for phasing in compact fluorescents room by room. Do at least one room immediately, starting with the room where you spend most of your time. Then complete at least one room a month and commit to finishing the project within a year. If you're inspired, consider doing your entire house at once!

MATERIALS
- Paper and pencil, compact fluorescents.

TIME
- 15 minutes to complete your home lighting survey and lighting plan; one hour or more to purchase the bulbs; 15 minutes to change a room's worth of lighting.

WEAR IT AGAIN SAM

WASHING AND DRYING CLOTHES EFFICIENTLY

Do your clothes really need to go to the laundry or the dry cleaners after a wearing or two, or will the simple touch of an iron or the removal of a dirty spot allow you to wear them again? Electric washers and dryers can account for as much as 25% of your home electricity use. This Earth Action will help our Earth while saving you money.

EARTH ACTION

- Wear clothes until they are actually dirty. Hang them up after each wearing to let them air out naturally.
- Use an iron to touch up creases, or a wet cloth and a little soap to get a spot out when the rest of the garment is clean.
- When you do wash and dry your clothes, do it in an energy-efficient manner:
  - Wash with cold water, which, contrary to popular opinion, gets most clothes just as clean as hot water. It will also save up to 85% of the energy costs associated with washing your clothes because you don't have to heat the water. Greasy stains may require hot water, but always rinse with cold water.
  - Make sure you wash a full load (but don't pack the tub).
  - Use a clothesline whenever possible and let nature get into the act. Unless your home has a humidity problem, a drying rack indoors works well in cold or inclement weather.
  - Clean your dryer's lint filter after each use and the exhaust hose periodically to allow air circulation that will enable the dryer to operate at maximum efficiency.
  - Dry full loads (but not overfilled).
- When you buy a new washer, get an Energy Star® rated front-loader. When you buy a new dryer, look for the Energy Star® label.

MATERIALS

- Iron, wet cloth and soap, clothesline, drying rack.

TIME

- A few minutes to iron, remove a spot, or hang clothes up to dry.

RESOURCE SAVINGS

You save energy, and if your utility company uses fossil fuels, you improve air quality and reduce global warming. Your clothes will last longer if they are washed less frequently in cold water and air dried. You will also save the resources and money necessary to replace them.

WELL, IT SURE IS NICE TO GET OUTSIDE!

YEAH, THE SUN FEELS GOOD!

MEET YOUR WATER HEATER

MAKING YOUR WATER HEATER MORE EFFICIENT

WHY ACT? You probably don't think about your water heater unless your shower turns cold. Your water heater, however, represents about 20% of the energy used in your home. Much of this is unnecessarily lost, especially if the heater was designed before 1989. This Earth Action will help you improve your water heating system so you heat the water and not the surrounding air.

RESOURCE SAVINGS

You save energy and money. For every 10° F you lower the water temperature, you will save 3-5% of the energy you use to heat water. If your water heater uses fossil fuels, you reduce air pollution and global warming as well. Your efforts help us all.

EARTH ACTION

This Earth Action has two parts: operation and insulation.

- To operate your water heating system for maximum efficiency:
  - Set the water temperature at 120° F. If the dial on your tank doesn't have temperature marks, use a thermometer (available from your hardware or camera store) to check the temperature of the hot water coming from your faucet. For each 10° F reduction, you'll save 3%-5% on your water heating bill. Have your water heater tuned up every few years to operate at maximum efficiency.
  - Turn your hot water setting to "off" or "pilot" when you go on a trip.
  - If you have an electric water heater, install a timer that will turn your water heater off midday and overnight.
- If your water heater does not already have adequate internal insulation:
  - Install an insulating blanket around your water heater. Especially if it is located in a garage or basement, this can save from 4% to 10% of the energy you've been using and pay for itself in 3-12 months depending on the kind of water heater you have. Most water heaters manufactured after 1989 have sufficient insulation.
  - Insulate hot water pipes with foam sleeves.
  - The above items may be provided at no cost by utility companies as part of a free home energy audit. They can also be purchased inexpensively from your local hardware store.
- Many utility companies give rebates to install new, more efficient water heaters. Inquire whether there is a rebate program in your area.

NOTE: If it is time to purchase a new water heater, be sure to buy one with the Energy Star® label, or if you want to go the extra mile and let the sun do the job, research whether a solar water heating system will work in your area.

MATERIALS

- Insulating blanket, insulating sleeves, thermometer, timer.

TIME

- 10-60 minutes, depending on what has to be done.

FRIDGE PHYSICAL

MAKING YOUR REFRIGERATOR MORE EFFICIENT

 Your fridge uses more electricity than any other appliance in your home, almost 25% of your total household appliance energy use. This Earth Action will help you get your refrigerator in shape.

EARTH ACTION

- If you have more than one refrigerator, try to get by using one. This could save you up to $150 a year.
- Check the tightness of the seal on your refrigerator door:
  - Visually inspect the rubber gasket to see if it is sealing well, or open the door, slide a piece of paper between the door seal and the fridge, then close the door. If the paper pulls out easily, the seal is not tight enough.
  - If the seal is not tight, use some self-stick weather stripping to create a better seal or, if necessary, replace the seal.
- Approximately twice a year, vacuum or wipe the condenser coils (at the back or behind the front grill—usually at the bottom) to remove dust so the coils operate efficiently.
- To use your refrigerator more efficiently:
  - The temperature should be about 38° F in the fridge and about 5° F in the freezer. Place a thermometer in the fridge and adjust the thermostat accordingly.
  - If your fridge has a "power miser" switch, use it.
  - Decide what you want before you open the door so you don't let warm air in.
- If you leave town for a week or two, empty the refrigerator of perishable items and put it on the lowest setting.

NOTE: If you have an old refrigerator, get an estimate from an appliance store or independent guidebook of the payback time associated with installing a new, super efficient model. Look for one with the Energy Star® label.

MATERIALS

- Paper, vacuum cleaner or rag, thermometer, weather stripping, replacement seal if needed.

TIME

- About 15 minutes twice a year; an hour to purchase and half an hour to replace the seal if necessary.

RESOURCE SAVINGS

You save energy, money, and reduce global warming if your utility company burns fossil fuels. Your effort is helping our planet!

BETTER A SWEATER
TURNING DOWN THE THERMOSTAT

WHY ACT? During cold weather, many people set the thermostat a little warmer than it needs to be. You can turn down the thermostat a little, still be comfortable, and make a big difference, since home heating accounts for over a quarter of your energy bill! This Earth Action will show you one of the simplest ways to save a great deal of energy and money, and if you are using fossil fuels, improve air quality.

RESOURCE SAVINGS

You save energy and money, and if your heating system uses fossil fuels, you improve air quality and reduce global warming.
You are making a difference in our world!

EARTH ACTION
• Call a meeting of your household. Ask for their cooperation. Agree on temperature settings and guidelines.
• During the day when people are home, set your thermostat at "sweater" temperature: somewhere between 65° F and 68° F.
• Before going to bed at night or when every one is out of the house, set the thermostat to "blanket" temperature: between 55° F and 58° F.
NOTE: Consider installing a programmable thermostat so you make sure the heat is always at the temperature you wish. This can reduce your heating bill by up to 20%. Look for an Energy Star® model.

MATERIALS
• Sweater or sweatshirt, warm blanket, programmable thermostat.

TIME
• A few minutes for the meeting; a few hours to purchase and install a programmable thermostat and a few seconds to set the thermostat.

FURNACE FLING

MAKING YOUR FURNACE MORE EFFICIENT

 If you live in a colder climate, one of the most important things you can do to save energy is to regularly tune up your furnace. Depending on where you live, up to 65% of the energy you use in your home goes to heat it. A heating system can waste 30%-50% of the energy it uses if it is not operating efficiently. This Earth Action will show you how to give your furnace the periodic tune-up it needs.

EARTH ACTION

Oil furnaces need a tune-up annually; gas furnaces should get one every two years.

- Call your furnace servicing company and schedule an appointment to have your furnace cleaned and adjusted. (Ask the service technician how often you should change your filter. If it is more often than your regular servicing, ask the technician to show you how to change it. Inquire about re-usable air filters.)
- Seal and insulate all warm-air heating ducts that pass through unheated areas such as crawl spaces. This can improve the efficiency of your heating system by as much as 30%. Your furnace servicing company can do the work. Ask the company for instructions if you choose to do it yourself. It's a relatively simple process. For safety reasons, be sure the technician performs a backdrafting test on your fireplace and gas or oil furnace after sealing ducts.

NOTE: If you have an old furnace, get a free estimate of the payback time associated with installing a new, higher efficiency model. Look for one with a high Energy Star® rating.

MATERIALS

- Phone, phone book, sealant, and insulation.

TIME

- Five minutes to select the company and make the appointment. More time if you're doing the work yourself.

RESOURCE SAVINGS

You save money and energy, and reduce global warming. Your efforts in this area make a real difference!

PUTTING ON AIRS

INSULATING WINDOWS AND DOORS

 WHY ACT? Remember the dress-in-layers-to-keep-warm principle? It works by trapping pockets of air that act as buffers between your warm body and the cold air around it. Think of the interior of your house as your warm body, and drapes, storm windows, shades, and blinds as the layers that keep you warm. Windows are responsible for 10%-25% of a home's heat loss, adding $50-$125 to the average annual heating bill. This Earth Action will show you how to save energy whether you rent or own your home.

RESOURCE SAVINGS

You save the money you would have spent to heat escaping air, and you reduce air pollution and reduce global warming. Storm windows can cut heat loss by 25%-50%. An uninsulated drape can reduce 30% of the heat being lost through a window; an insulated drape can cut it by up to 50%. Your effort is time well spent for you and the Earth.

EARTH ACTION

- Insulate the glass in your home. Here's how:
  - Do a survey of all your windows and glass doors, noting whether they have storm windows, single-, double-, triple-pane or "low-emissivity" glass, insulated or noninsulated drapes, shades or blinds.
  - Measure each window or glass door that needs more layers.
  - Call a storm window installer, window supplier or shop that sells window insulation or makes drapes, shades, and blinds. Price the cost of having these items made for your windows and glass doors, including the cost to have insulated material added to existing drapes. Estimate payback time for this investment. If you are purchasing new windows, be sure to buy ones with the Energy Star® rating.
  - Based on this information, create a long-term plan for window insulation. Consider starting with the room in which you spend the most time.
- If you rent your home or apartment, meet with your landlord and explain the benefits of this financial investment. You might also volunteer to do some of the work in return for a rent reduction.
- If money is an issue, consider doing these less expensive upgrades:
  - You can make low-cost thermal shades from an insulating material such as Reflectix, available by the roll at a home supply store.
  - You can also install plastic barriers, available in kits from a home supply store, on the insides of your windows and glass doors. Although temporary, plastic is the least expensive alternative, at a cost of about $2 per window, and will cut heat loss through single-pane windows by 25%-40%.

MATERIALS

- Storm windows; double- or triple-pane windows, drapes, drapery insulating material, shades, blinds, or clear plastic.

TIME

- Half an hour to conduct your window and door survey; two hours or less to price the items; more time to make, order, or install them.

CHILL OUT

ADDING WEATHER STRIPPING AND CAULKING—GETTING AN ENERGY AUDIT

 Did you know that air leaks in the typical American home are equivalent to leaving an average-size window open all the time. These air leaks are found around windows and doors, along heating ducts, around plumbing pipes and fireplaces. This represents as much as a 15% loss of the energy you use to heat your home. That's a big hole in your pocket! Even if you are a renter, you may be paying for heat and living with uncomfortable drafts in your home.

EARTH ACTION

- Call your local utility company to see if it conducts free energy audits. It may include free air-sealing materials. Energy audits may also be available from independant contractors, non-profits, and government agencies.
- If an energy audit is not available, or you prefer to do it yourself, here's how:
  - Determine where to seal by feeling around doors, windows, electrical and plumbing outlets, and cracks where cold air may be coming in. You can place a candle or lighted incense stick near the area to help indicate an air leak in cold weather.
- Purchase and install, as needed, the following inexpensive items from your local hardware store: weather stripping, outlet insulators (precut insulating material that fits behind the switch plates), "sweeps" designed for the bottoms of doors and attic access hatches, window putty to seal window panes, and caulking, which may be adequate for some cracks. These items only cost a few dollars and will begin saving you money on your energy bill within the first year. If you are a tenant, see if you can work out a plan with your landlord to deduct the cost from your rent.

NOTE: To take this farther, refer to "Farther Down the Path: A Sustainable Energy Household" on page 60.

MATERIALS

- Weather stripping, outlet insulators, door sweeps, window putty, and caulking.

TIME

- Up to two hours to do audit and another few hours for simple low-cost improvements.

RESOURCE SAVINGS

You save money you were spending for wasted energy, improve air quality, and reduce global warming by reducing your use of fossil fuels. As you plug up holes in your home, you are securing our planet's future.

EVERY DOOR SHOULD HAVE ONE OF THESE!

CHILL IN
COOLING YOUR HOUSE MORE EFFICIENTLY

WHY ACT? If you use air conditioning, you may be overcooling your home or apartment beyond what you need to be comfortable. This Earth Action will help you cool your home in a way that provides you and the planet comfort.

RESOURCE SAVINGS

You save money and energy, and if your utility company burns fossil fuels, you improve air quality and reduce global warming. Now that's being cool!

EARTH ACTION
- When installing your air conditioner:
  - For the most efficient model, look for one with an Energy Star® rating.
  - Make sure the unit is the correct size for the amount of space you are cooling and, if possible, install the unit in the shade to reduce the workload.
  - If your air conditioner must be in the sun, build a protective shade or screen over it. Make sure this does not block air circulation. This increases the unit's efficiency by 5%-10%.
- To maintain your air conditioner:
  - Inspect the filter every month during cooling seasons. Clean and replace the filter when needed. A clogged filter can use 5% more energy than a clean one. Clean the entire unit at least once a year, according to the manufacturer's instructions.
  - If you have a central air-conditioning system, have it tuned up and the coils cleaned every 3 years. Regular servicing of a central air system can yield a 10%-20% energy savings.
- To effectively operate your air conditioner:
  - Set your thermostat at "short sleeve" temperature: 78° F. If the temperature outside is the same or cooler than that, just open the windows. If you have an older air conditioner that does not have the temperatures marked on the dial, use a room thermometer. For every degree you raise the thermostat, you save 3%-5% of your cooling costs.
  - Install a timer on your room air conditioner or an Energy Star® rated programmable thermostat for your central air-conditioning system so you don't have to leave it on when it's not needed. It's a myth that it's more efficient to leave an air conditioner on than to shut it off and have to recool a home later. It pays to turn off your air conditioner when you will be gone for more than an hour.
  - If you don't wish to use an air conditioner or you want to reduce the amount of energy your air conditioner uses, consider keeping your shades or curtains drawn during the heat of the day and planting trees on the western, southern, and eastern sides of your house. A home's indoor temperature can rise as much as 20° F if the windows are not shaded.

MATERIALS
- Materials for protective shades, filters, vacuum cleaner, timer, or programmable thermostat.

TIME
- Five minutes to clean your filter periodically; five minutes to make an appointment to have it serviced professionally; some more time to do the job yourself.

FANS ARE COOL

USING FANS TO COOL YOUR HOME

Air conditioning uses up to 15% of a household's energy expenditures, which can be as much as $300 per year. Producing electricity from fossil fuels creates pollution and contributes to global warming. Staying cool is cheaper and causes far less pollution if you use fans instead. This Earth Action will help you keep your cool.

EARTH ACTION

- A breeze helps cool your skin, so use fans to circulate the air in your home.
- When the temperature goes down at night, use fans in windows to direct cooler air in and flush warm air out. This works best if you pull air in at the lowest level and push it out at the highest level of your living space.
- Better yet, you can install a special device called a whole house fan in the ceiling of your top floor to push large amounts of warm air up and out. If you install a whole house fan, make sure there is a way to seal it up and insulate it during the winter.

MATERIALS

- Circular or box fan(s), or a whole house fan

TIME

- A few minutes to set up fans

RESOURCE SAVINGS

You save energy, money and reduce global warming from power plants - a triple play!

WHAT YOU SEE IS WHAT YOU BREATHE
PREVENTING AIR POLLUTION

WHY ACT? Certain weather conditions, when combined with pollution from cars and other gasoline-powered engines, can create dangerous levels of ozone and smog. Smog is especially harmful to the lungs of children, seniors, people with chronic lung problems like asthma, and those who exercise vigorously outdoors. Poor air quality also causes eye, nose and throat irritations, and reduces resistance to lung infections and colds.

RESOURCE SAVINGS

You reduce air pollution and reduce global warming. If we each do our part, we can improve and preserve our planet for future generations. We all will thank you!

EARTH ACTION
- The first step is to be a weather watcher to determine when we are experiencing poor air quality. In the winter, look for still, cold and hazy days; in warmer months, look for still, hot, and hazy days. Many communities have a local air quality information line. Find out if your area has one. You can also check the EPA's AirNow Website www.epa.gov/airnow.
- If there is poor air quality, or a smog alert in your community, do the following:
  - Avoid or minimize use of gasoline powered equipment, including cars, trucks, boats, and lawn or garden tools. Walk, bike, telecommute, use public transportation, and take the day off from lawn and garden care, or use electric lawn and garden equipment.
  - Refuel your car, boat, or gasoline powered equipment in the cooler evening hours. This will help reduce the amount of gasoline vapors that can contribute to daytime smog.
  - If you have a woodstove or fireplace, minimize its use unless it is your only source of heat. If you have to burn, burn compressed sawdust logs, pellets, or very dry firewood. Dry wood burns hot and produces less smoke.
  - Use alternatives to outdoor burning, such as chipping and composting your yard waste. Always curtail burning if there is a burn ban. Call your local fire department to find out about burn regulations.

NOTE: Never burn garbage, plastic, rubber or treated wood. Not only is it extremely toxic to the environment—it's illegal!

MATERIALS
- Phone, bike, walking shoes, lunch box, electric lawn and garden equipment, muscle-powered water sports equipment.

TIME
- A minute or two to find out about current air quality.

RELATING TO NATURE: AN ENLIGHTENING EXPERIENCE

WATCHING THE SUNRISE

WHY ACT? The Sun lights your way, keeps you warm, and provides the plants you eat with the energy they require. A calm, quiet feeling comes over most people as they watch a sunrise, yet how many of us take time to experience one of the most awesome moments of the day: nature's awakening? To start your day with the dawn is a profound sensation and one that's always different since no two sunrises are entirely alike. This Earth Action will help you to appreciate the Sun, the original source of all the energy you use in life.

EARTH ACTION
- Check the newspaper to see what time the Sun rises.
- If you can, find an open area — or a rooftop — where you will be able to see the Sun as it breaks over the horizon. Arrange to go with a friend or two so you can enjoy the sunrise together.
- Bring a camera and take a picture of the sunrise, write a poem as you experience the moment, or if you'd prefer, read a poem about the Sun written by another admirer. Choose the poem in advance and bring it with you.

NOTE: You may want to keep your photograph or your poem in a special place as a reminder of the Sun's majesty.

MATERIALS
- Newspaper, open area or rooftops, camera, paper and pen, book of poems.

TIME
- About half an hour of eternity.

*NOTE: When watching the sunrise, be sure not to look directly into the sun to avoid damage to your eyes.

RESOURCE SAVINGS

None. But after watching nature rouse herself, you may come to feel differently about how you use her precious resources. And you'll take away a cheery feeling as you begin your own day.

FARTHER DOWN THE PATH:

WHY ACT? Using energy efficiently and using those forms of energy that the Earth can renew are the principles of creating a sustainable energy household. One starts by doing the easy and inexpensive things such as remembering to turn off the lights, weather-stripping windows and doors, and taking advantage of the sun for lighting and heating whenever possible. This action invites you to go farther down the path—achieving maximum energy efficiency and shifting to renewable energy sources.

RESOURCE SAVINGS

You reduce the amount of air pollutants and greenhouse gases such as CO_2 you generate. You are also supporting the long-term shift of society from an unsustainable to a sustainable energy path.

ACTION continued on next page

A SUSTAINABLE ENERGY HOUSEHOLD

EARTH ACTION:

- Begin by becoming knowledgeable about where your house is on the path of energy-efficiency and renewable energy alternatives.
- Contact an energy expert and get an on-site audit (see "Chill Out", p. 55). Considering the financial investments you will be making, you are well served to pay for expert professional advice. You will want to supplement this audit by getting special advice about your heating system from a heating technician (generally offered as part of a yearly tune-up). An excellent source of information about energy efficiency is the book *Homemade Money*, by Richard Heede.
- Inquire whether the local electric utility currently offers or plans to offer "green power" (solar, hydro, wind, biomass, geothermal, etc.). If they don't, deregulation may allow you to buy it from other utilities that offer this service in your area. A premium is charged for this energy service which can be offset by cost savings from greater energy efficiency.
- Ask your energy expert which renewable energy technologies would make sense for your house. If they don't have this expertise ask for a recommendation of someone locally who does, or do your own research. If you are unsuccessful in your local research, or wish supplemental information contact: Energy Efficiency and Renewable Energy Clearinghouse at 800-363-3732, (www.eere.energy.gov). They can provide you with a number of free publications, including how to do your own energy audit. They are funded by the US Department of Energy. Your state energy office can provide information about any energy efficiency financial incentive programs for which you might qualify.
- Based on what you've learned from your audit and research, you're now ready to develop a long-term plan for maximizing the energy efficiency and renewable energy use of your home. A few things to keep in mind:
  - The highest priority is to fully weatherize your house, which includes insulation of attics, walls, and foundation areas and reducing air leaks.
  - Keep heating equipment tuned up. When replacing, have the contractor calculate the life-cycle benefits of various equipment and fuels.
  - When replacing appliances, compare yellow Energy Guide labels and choose those that operate in the top 10% of efficiency for their size and class.
  - In calculating the cost/benefit of a particular energy efficiency option or renewable energy technology, include the payback period (or lifecycle costs for items over $1,000), comfort, environmental impact, convenience, and current investment budget.
- Make a three-to-five year plan detailing year one, along with a budget. Some of the easy-to-do actions described in this section can be done immediately. And do remember that your daily energy saving practices are an integral part of creating a sustainable energy household.

MATERIALS
- Paper, pen, telephone, yellow pages.

TIME
- Three to five hours. An hour to research energy experts, an hour or two to review the findings of the audit, an hour or two to create your long-term plan, and time to take the first action.

5

ACTION NOTES

ACTION NOTES

_____
_____
_____
_____
_____
_____
_____
_____
_____
_____
_____
_____
_____
_____
_____
_____
_____
_____
_____
_____
_____
_____
_____
_____

ACTION NOTES

TICKET TO RIDE—ACTION LOG

Actions	Action Plan		Discussed with Household	Action Done	Points
Getting There on Your Own Steam	Day:	Time:	☐	☐	2
Energy x Mass = a Healthier Earth	Day:	Time:	☐	☐	3
A Good Deed	Day:	Time:	☐	☐	2
R & R: Relax & Ride	Day:	Time:	☐	☐	3
The Road Not Taken	Day:	Time:	☐	☐	3.
Drive Earth-Smart	Day:	Time:	☐	☐	2
Don't Be An Oil Drip	Day:	Time:	☐	☐	4
Is Your Car Physically Fit?	Day:	Time:	☐	☐	2
Befriend an Earth-Smart Auto	Day:	Time:	☐	☐	3
Vacation with the Earth	Day:	Time:	☐	☐	2
Relating to Nature: Smell the Flowers	Day:	Time:	☐	☐	1
Farther Down the Path: Reducing Vehicle Miles Traveled	Day:	Time:	☐	☐	6

STEP 4

TICKET TO RIDE

TRANSPORTATION EFFICIENCY

TRANSPORTATION AND YOU

Freedom is a quality that Americans value almost more than anything else. Mobility is the epitome of freedom, and the car is its symbol. It allows us to go where we want, when we want. This freedom is not enjoyed by the majority of people in other parts of the world, where a car, and even a good quality road, is a luxury. This freedom of mobility, however, presents us with a dilemma: The gasoline that fuels our vehicles costs more than its price per gallon.

Most gasoline comes from fossil fuel which, when burned, causes air pollution and becomes a major contributor to acid rain and global warming. As you might have guessed, since we Americans are not well-versed in using resources efficiently, we use gasoline wastefully. This inefficiency also translates into wasteful spending and, in the case of commuting and routine errands, wasted time as well.

There are positive alternatives in transportation that will allow you to maintain or improve your quality of life while more efficiently stewarding the fossil fuels you use. This section will help you develop sustainable transportation practices. It can even provide you with enough time to smell the flowers along the road. Here's to planet-friendly travel!

GETTING THERE ON YOUR OWN STEAM
WALKING AND BIKING TO DESTINATIONS

Did you know there's a simple way to improve air quality and reduce the amount of fossil fuel your car requires? Just switch to a different type of energy: your own steam! Bicycling and walking are the two most energy efficient forms of travel on the planet. This Earth Action will help you become part of a new trend in America, one that has long since taken hold in European countries such as the Netherlands and Denmark: walking and bicycling.

EARTH ACTION
- Review the places you usually drive to each week. Think of routes where you could regularly walk or bicycle instead. In certain locations, you may even be able to cross-country ski or roller blade.
- Substitute at least one regularly traveled route each week with a means of transportation powered by you. Bring a backpack to carry your belongings, purchases, or papers.
  - If you use a bicycle or roller blades in the street, take safety precautions and follow traffic codes.
- Encourage a friend or co-worker along your route to join you. You'll catch up on the latest news and double the improvement in air quality.
- Look for other opportunities, as they arise, to walk or bicycle instead of drive.

MATERIALS
- A good pair of walking or running shoes, a bicycle, cross-country skis, or roller blades, backpack, and a water bottle.

TIME
- 15 minutes to review the places you normally drive to that you could reach on your own steam.
- Depending on your destination, you may need to allow some extra time to get there on your own steam.

RESOURCE SAVINGS

You improve the quality of the air we all breathe, save money, and reduce global warming. As you become more physically fit, you also make the air healthier for all living creatures and the water purer for fish. Your simple effort is a great act of kindness to our Earth.

ENERGY X MASS: A HEALTHIER EARTH
USING PUBLIC TRANSPORTATION

WHY ACT? It's easy to be an Einstein and understand the relationship between energy and mass: mass transit is more energy efficient, reduces fuel emissions, and improves air quality. Think about how many miles per gallon your car gets. Compare that to the 110 passenger-miles per gallon an intracity bus gets! This Earth Action will show you how leaving the driving to someone else can enable you to help our planet while you catch up on your work, reading, or dreaming.

RESOURCE SAVINGS

You improve air quality, save gasoline, and reduce global warming. One full 40 foot bus will take 58 cars off the road; a six car passenger train can take 900 cars off the road. You're making the world better for everyone!

EARTH ACTION
- Make a list of the routes you commonly travel, such as commuting to work.
- Research whether public transportation can get you there instead. Find out schedules, frequency, and cost.
- Replace at least one regularly traveled route you now drive with public transportation.
- As new trips are added, research whether you can get there by public transportation instead, and make an effort to do so.

NOTE: At some time, you may also want to consider getting rid of one of your cars—if you have more than one—now that you are using mass transit some of the time. You will not only save money for maintenance, insurance, and gasoline but also get money for selling it. This money can be used for vacations and other pleasant things, or just to buy yourself some time.

MATERIALS
- Paper and pen, mass transit schedules.

TIME
- An hour to gather schedules and make your transportation plan. After that, you can gain time to do other things while riding mass transit instead of driving.

THE ENERGY BUS

THANKS FOR TAKING OVER!

NO PROBLEM!

4

A GOOD DEED
COMBINING TRIPS

With increased awareness and planning, you can reduce the amount of driving you have to do. This Earth Action will help you cut back on the number of trips required for your errands and free up time in your life. Enjoy this time!

EARTH ACTION

- Gather household members and ask them to play an ongoing game with you. The game is called: "How Much Can We Get Done While Using the Least Amount of Gasoline, Money and Time?" For short, let's call it: "Green Time!" This is how it's played:
  - With household members, or on your own if you live by yourself, review each week in advance and consider all the errands for which a car will be needed.
  - Combine whichever ones you can that involve destinations near one another.
  - As new errands are needed, try to combine them with other trips as well.
- Each time you are planning to run an errand, get into the habit of asking household members if they need anything from the same place, or along the way where you are going.

MATERIALS

- Paper, pen, your new awareness reminding you to ask others if they need something.

TIME

- 10 minutes to plan your errands each week; new time to do whatever you like as a result of combining trips.

RESOURCE SAVINGS

You improve air quality and reduce global warming by reducing fuel emissions, and save yourself money and time. You've turned what could have been a chore—doing errands—into a good deed for others and our planet! You win. And so does everyone else!

R & R: RELAX & RIDE

CARPOOLING

WHY ACT? The logic of carpools is simple: for every two people who share a car, you can cut energy use and air pollution in half! With four riders, you can reduce it to a quarter. How often could you be sharing a car with others who are going to the same place—or in the same direction—whether it's work; kids' after-school activities; committee meetings; a restaurant, party, or friend's home; a baseball game; or the gym? While helping the planet, this Earth Action will help you free up time from driving to spend in more relaxing and productive ways. Enjoy using it to chat, nap, work, read, or daydream.

RESOURCE SAVINGS

You improve air quality, reduce global warming, and save wear and tear on your car. You are also showing the children in your carpool that you care about the world in which they are growing up. Each time someone else in your carpool does the driving, relax and enjoy the ride. You've earned it!

EARTH ACTION

• Join or form a carpool. Here's how:
  - Make a list of the regular trips in your week where you could carpool rather than drive alone, such as work commutes, after-school activities for the kids, a club gathering, or service organization meeting.
  - Ask your manager, employer, or group leader for help in facilitating a carpool at the next opportunity.
  - Follow up by speaking to these people at work, in your neighborhood, or at the event and establish a regular carpool.
  - Many cities and regions have special agencies to help arrange carpooling, and some even provide free carpool vans. Call your local government, or look in your Yellow Pages.
• As opportunities arise where you can take one car instead of several—such as going to a restaurant or musical event—arrange to travel with others.

MATERIALS

• Paper and pen, Yellow Pages and phone, new or old friends or colleagues, one car.

TIME:

• 20 minutes to establish each carpool.

THE ROAD NOT TAKEN
TELECOMMUTING/ALTERNATIVE WORK SCHEDULES

Telecommuting—working from a home office that is connected electronically to a business office—is a great way to be close to family members during working hours. It will also save you time and money and improve air quality for all of us by decreasing the number of cars on the road. This Earth Action will show you how to let your fingers do the driving instead, with a computer, modem, fax machine, and phone.

EARTH ACTION
- Arrange to work from home:
  - If you have a job that could be done at home, explore the possibilities with your employer and members of your household. Arrange to work from home at least one day a week.
  - Or, if you are self-employed and could do part or all of your work from home, create a plan, again working at home at least one day a week and as much as possible.
  - Either way, establish an office or office space in your home with any electronic equipment you will need: computer, modem, fax machine, and phone.
- Try tele-shopping and doing other errands using your phone or the Internet.
- Consider tele-schooling, many colleges and universities offer accredited courses you can take via the Internet.

NOTE: When you consider moving, try moving closer to work to reduce your commute.

MATERIALS
- Computer, modem, fax machine, phone.

TIME
- One hour to meet with your employer or manager. After that, you gain time. All the time you no longer spend commuting is more free time to spend with family and friends, enjoy recreational activities, or sleep later.

RESOURCE SAVINGS

If you telecommute one day per week per year (based on a 20-mile round trip commute) you can save up to $500 in operating costs and have the equivalent of about 25 hours of added free time. You would also prevent about 1,000 pounds of CO_2, a principal cause of global warming, from entering the atmosphere. Nice going!

3

DRIVE EARTH-SMART

DEVELOPING FUEL-EFFICIENT DRIVING HABITS

 Did you know you can save gasoline, the air pollution it causes, and 10%-30% of your car's fuel costs just by driving smart? This Earth Action will not only improve the quality of the air we all breathe, and save you money, but also encourage you to drive more safely.

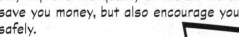

You improve air quality, reduce global warming, and save gasoline and money. While you are helping to make our environment cleaner, you are also making it safer. You're letting the Earth—and those living on it—know how much you care.

EARTH ACTION

Here's how to drive smart:

- Before you even pull out of the driveway:
  - If your household has more than one vehicle, always drive the more fuel-efficient model if you have a choice.
  - Plan your route, including commutes to work. The best route may not be the shortest, but the one that prevents idling in traffic. In city driving, up to one-third of a fuel's potential energy can be wasted through idling.
  - Rid your car of any unnecessary weight. You lose about 1% of fuel efficiency for every extra 100 pounds.
  - Minimize cold starts and limit warmups to 30 seconds.
- When driving on the highway:
  - Maintain a steady speed, using your cruise control device if you have one. While 55 mph may no longer be the speed limit, it's still the most fuel-efficient highway speed and will save you up to 30% in fuel costs compared with driving at 75 mph. It's also safer.
  - Keep windows closed for better aerodynamics, which, in turn, saves fuel.
- When driving on secondary roads:
  - Anticipate stops and slowdowns. Accelerate, decelerate, and brake steadily to save gas.
  - When appropriate, drive between 35 and 45 mph, the most fuel-efficient range.
  - Save gasoline at bank drive-through windows and fast-food restaurants by not using them if there is a long line of cars ahead of you. Park and go inside instead.
  - Consider turning off your car engine when your car is stopped for a minute or two, as when waiting for a train to pass.
- Limit short trips. Most of the particulate pollution that a car generates occurs in the first few miles. For short trips, a bike may be faster anyway.

MATERIALS

- A light foot on the pedal.

TIME

- No time at all.

DON'T BE AN OIL DRIP

IDENTIFYING AND PLUGGING OIL LEAKS ON YOUR VEHICLE

 Oil and other fluids that leak from your car are washed from the street into tributaries and storm drains that flow directly into our streams and waterways. In the U.S., it is estimated that petroleum washed off pavement every year, along with oil dumped into storm drains, sends 15 times more oil into the ocean than the Exxon Valdez did. This Earth Action will help you reduce harmful oil runoff from your vehicle.

EARTH ACTION

This Earth Action has two parts - check for oil leaks and fix them.

- Before you drive away, simply back up one car length and check the ground for any oil leaks where you were parked.
- If you find an oil leak, call your local repair shop to fix it, or make a plan to repair it as soon as possible. Consider using recycled oil.
  - Clean up spills immediately. You can purchase a non-toxic, biodegradable chemical that will safely break down oil deposits from your local home supply or boat marine store. If you can't find this, consider using kitty litter to soak up oil. Place in garbage can in a sealed bag.
  - When parked in your driveway, keep a drip pan under the leak until you repair it. Empty the collected fluids into a tightly sealed container and recycle.
- Use alternative transportation actions: carpool, bus, light rail, bicycle or skate.

NOTE: For boat owners: Look around the waterline for leaks or spills before leaving the dock. Always check for oil leaks inside the bilge before draining. If you discover a leak, call your local repair shop to fix it or make a plan to repair it as soon as possible.

MATERIALS

- Phone number of a local mechanic, drip pan, biodegradable material to break down the oil leak, plastic sealable container.

TIME

- A minute to check for leaks, more time for repairs.

RESOURCE SAVINGS

You reduce hazardous oil from draining into local water sources, protecting natural habitats, wildlife and water from contamination. One pint of motor oil can contaminate 125,000 gallons of drinking water and make an oil slick about the size of two football fields. Your efforts make a difference.

IS YOUR CAR PHYSICALLY FIT?

TUNE-UPS AND MAINTENANCE FOR YOUR CAR

 Did you know it's easy to increase your car's fuel efficiency? One of the most important things you can do is to keep your car in shape. A tuned car gets up to 40% better gas mileage than one that isn't. The less gasoline you burn, the more you improve the quality of the air we breathe. This Earth Action will help you keep the tiger in your tank purring!

RESOURCE SAVINGS

You improve air quality, save money, and lessen the demand for fossil fuels. Each gallon of gas your car doesn't use prevents the emmission of about 20 pounds of carbon dioxide, the principal cause of global warming. Your action helps us all breathe easier!

EARTH ACTION
- Have your car serviced on a regular basis.
  - Consult a car mechanic or refer to your vehicle's owner's manual and begin an appropriate maintenance schedule.
  - If you are due for servicing, make an appointment.
  - When filling your tank, don't buy a higher octane gas than your engine needs.
  - Buy a tire gauge and use it periodically. Inflate your tires to the pressure that is printed on them. Always check and adjust the pressure when the tires are cold. If your tires are underinflated even a few pounds per square inch, which is not uncommon, your fuel costs could increase by as much as 5%.

MATERIALS
- Car owner's manual, tire gauge.

TIME
- 10 minutes to study the owner's manual or call your car mechanic to determine when you need to have your car serviced; 5 minutes to make an appointment; a minute or two to check your tires every now and then.

BEFRIEND AN EARTH-SMART AUTO
RESEARCHING A FUEL-EFFICIENT VEHICLE

 WHY ACT? If you are considering purchasing a new car in the near future, this is an important action for you to take. You can make a dramatic improvement in your impact on global warming and save a considerable amount of money by purchasing a car that burns gasoline more efficiently. Domestic and imported models have an average fuel efficiency of about 23 miles per gallon, but cars are available that get over 50 mpg! This Earth Action will help you select a car that can serve your needs and those of the Earth at the same time.

EARTH ACTION
- Once you've determined your driving needs, purchase the most energy-efficient car possible. Here's how:
  - At the dealer showroom, check the fuel economy label affixed to the window for the model's average mpg, the estimated annual fuel cost, and the fuel economy range for other models in the same class. Compare the figures to those of other manufacturers using the Environmental Protection Agency's free gas mileage guide that dealers are required to provide.
  - Purchase the lightest vehicle you can, keeping in mind that every option adds weight. Get a cruise control device that will save gas by helping you maintain a steady speed on the highway. Studies have shown that vehicle design is more important in terms of safety than its weight and size.
  - Look for a streamlined design to reduce aerodynamic drag and improve fuel-efficiency.

NOTE: Consider a new breed of car that has significantly higher fuel efficiency or alternative fuels. The future of automobile efficiency will be changing for the better over the next years.

MATERIALS
- EPA gas mileage guide (available at dealerships); some good comparative shopping skills.

TIME
- A Saturday afternoon or two.

RESOURCE SAVINGS

A more efficient vehicle will save you energy and money and reduce global warming. Choosing a model that gets 10 mpg more can easily save $2,500 in fuel costs per year. That money can extend quite a few vacations or add to the quality of your life in other ways. Have fun in your Earth-friendly auto.

VACATION WITH THE EARTH
FUEL-EFFICIENT VACATION PLANNING

 Your vacation will be a time of renewal for you and the Earth if you minimize the use of your car to get to your destination and after you have arrived. A vacation, which allows you to walk or bike, will improve air quality by using less gasoline. This Earth Action will allow you to spend less time on the highway and in your car and more time experiencing the restorative power of nature's own sights and sounds.

RESOURCE SAVINGS

You improve air quality, reduce global warming and lessen wear and tear on your vehicle. At your vacation site, you are also likely to meet new people and see things by foot or bicycle you would have missed closed up in a car. Bon voyage!

EARTH ACTION
- Plan your next vacation with household members or other traveling partners.
  - Think of different kinds of vacations you can take that are close to home or reachable by public transportation.
  - If you are driving, try to find a destination that is within a one-day drive.
  - Look for places where you can get around primarily on your own steam by walking or riding bicycles.
  - For forays to the store, bring backpacks to carry your purchases.
  - Consider doing recreational activities — such as hiking, swimming, bicycling, or walking — that limit your need for motorized transportation.

MATERIALS
- Travel brochures and maps to plan your vacation. Once you have reached your destination, you may want to have bicycle(s), good walking or running shoes, and recreational gear for swimming, hiking, and other leisure pursuits.

TIME
- 60 minutes to plan your vacation.

RELATING TO NATURE: SMELL THE FLOWERS

WALKING IN NATURE

 When was the last time you took off on your own steam into the woods just to smell the flowers, see the birds, or dillydally along a lazy trail? It's rejuvenating to slow down and savor time, instead of racing about as we do in our vehicles. This Earth Action will help you get out of your car and become familiar with nature's rhythms.

EARTH ACTION

- Plan a hike or an outing to a wilderness area or local park. Ask a friend or household member to join you.
- Take along a backpack containing lunch packed in your BYO kit (See "Bring Your Own" p.7.), binoculars if you want to observe the birds, and a camera or drawing pad if you care to preserve the memory.
- During your walk, take the time to notice how different things look, sound, and smell when you are surrounded by nature. Stop and appreciate whatever trees, flowers, vistas, or animals give you pleasure. Each has its secret. You are guaranteed to bring away something special.

MATERIALS

- Walking shoes, BYO kit, binoculars (optional), camera or drawing pad (optional), keen senses.

TIME

- An afternoon.

RESOURCE SAVINGS

The real benefit here is your heightened awareness of how good it feels when you allow yourself to slow down and be in the present moment instead of rushing through life.

FARTHER DOWN THE PATH:

WHY ACT? The amount of vehicle miles traveled (VMT) per household is increasing dramatically every year which in turn is causing a significant environmental impact. In many cities and towns, auto emissions are the largest single source of air pollution. Highway construction and the sprawling development associated with it expand into farmland, wetlands and other undeveloped areas thus contributing to species extinction and the decline of open space. And the more miles we drive our car, the more we contribute to global warming and the depletion of our non-renewable energy resources. Many describe unconstrained automobile use as the greatest environmental problem facing our cities and towns today. Perhaps the greatest single step you can take toward sustainable living is to reduce the amount of single occupancy vehicle miles you travel each year. This action will support you in this endeavor.

EARTH ACTION

- Start by inviting each household member who drives a car to join you in this learning experience. Have each driver keep an automobile trip diary for two typical weeks. Note the destination and mileage of each trip. Divide the trips into different categories including: combinable, recreational, and other modes available (bus, bike, walking, car/van pool).
- At the end of two weeks add up the miles traveled by you and the other members of your household in each category. Project this over a year including any trips you normally take that didn't fall into this two-week period.
- Now the fun begins. Utilizing the Earth Actions described earlier in this section, create a plan to reduce your household's single occupancy vehicle miles traveled by between 20% and 50% over the next year. With forethought and careful planning, these goals are achievable for most people. What's needed is the creativity. You might be motivated by increasing the amount of time in your life, saving money, or seeing this as creating a personal environmental legacy to future generations. As part of your plan, write your motivation, and the benefits you hope to achieve from taking this action.
- Following are some examples of how you might choose your VMT reduction target.
  - Work: Telecommuting, carpooling, riding public transportation, walking or biking one day each week will reduce your commute VMT by 20%, two days a week by 40%.
  - Food shopping and household errands: Going twice as long between routine errands by making a list and buying in larger quantities could reduce VMT in this category by as much as 50% a week.
  - Children's school and after school activities: Carpooling with other parents could reduce this category of VMT by 20% to 80%.
- If you evaluate each typical trip this way, you will be amazed at what is possible with relatively little effort and forethought! Most of us are just habituated to our autos as our primary means of mobility. With a little creativity and effort to make the initial change, we will soon get just as habituated to a more environmentally sustainable means of transportation.

ACTION continued on next page

REDUCING VEHICLE MILES TRAVELED

NOTE: An idea that has become popular in a number of European cities and is now capturing the imagination of sustainability-minded US urban dwellers is car sharing. Instead of owning a car, or buying a second one, you participate in a community car sharing program and pay an annual fee and service charge each time you use the car. The financial savings and VMT reduction are significant. For more information: www.carsharing.net.

MATERIALS
Your automobile, pen, paper, creativity, bike, walking shoes, bus pass, etc.

TIME
A minute or so each car trip for two weeks to record your mileage. Two to three hours to create your VMT reduction plan. Significantly more free time for other things through your increased transportation efficiency.

RESOURCE SAVINGS
You extend the life expectancy of your car and the roads, improve air quality, and reduce your contribution to global warming. Also, for every mile less traveled, you have that much more money to spend on other things.

GOOD BUYS ARE FOREVER—ACTION LOG

Actions	Action Plan		Discussed with Household	Action Done	Points
Vote for the Earth	Day:	Time:	☐	☐	3
Think Before You Buy	Day:	Time:	☐	☐	3
Toxic Sleuth	Day:	Time:	☐	☐	3
A Breath fo Fresh Air	Day:	Time:	☐	☐	3
Home Sweet Home	Day:	Time:	☐	☐	2
What Goes Around Came Around	Day:	Time:	☐	☐	2
Vegetable Soup	Day:	Time:	☐	☐	2
Near and Dear	Day:	Time:	☐	☐	2
Chew On This for Awhile	Day:	Time:	☐	☐	3
Swap Party	Day:	Time:	☐	☐	2
Loan On Me	Day:	Time:	☐	☐	1
A Green Gardener	Day:	Time:	☐	☐	4
Relating to Nature: When the "Gotta Have Its" Attack, Head for the Garden	Day:	Time:	☐	☐	1
Farther Down the Path: A Sustainable Lifestyle	Day:	Time:	☐	☐	6

STEP 5 GOOD BUYS ARE FOREVER
ECO-WISE CONSUMING

CONSUMPTION AND YOU

Being American has allowed us access to an extraordinary assortment of goods and services to make our lives easier and more enjoyable. Our society has encouraged us to freely partake of this material bounty, and many of us have. However, as our planet reaches its resource limits, we must learn how to live within the means of the Earth. Simultaneously, many of us are reaching the limits of what a material existence can offer and are seeking to simplify our lives. Americans have embarked upon both an external and an internal search for a change of ways.

Once again the ethic of responsible stewardship of the planet's resources can serve as a guiding principle for how to develop sustainable consumption practices. The starting point of this practice is thoughtfulness. Before we buy something we need to ask ourselves, "Why am I buying this? Is there a way to fulfill this need without using the Earth's precious resources?" When we do buy something, we need to look for items that are produced and packaged in as environmentally responsible a manner as possible. When we have used up the product, it is our responsibility to look for ways to recycle it. Keeping these ideas in mind will allow us to make better choices.

Living a life of environmental stewardship requires that we educate both ourselves and the businesses from whom we buy. While only a small percentage of businesses are producing products in an environmentally responsible manner, more would if they were educated by their customers. The nature of business is to satisfy you as a customer. Buying environmentally responsible products and making specific requests to companies both go a long way in determining what gets produced. You are in a position of more influence than you might imagine. This section of your journey will enable you to develop the lifestyle practices of an eco-wise consumer.

VOTE FOR THE EARTH

BUYING EARTH-FRIENDLY PRODUCTS

 Did you know that you vote almost every day of your life, not just on election day? Each time you buy a product, you are casting a vote in favor of the materials and processes used to make it, the way it is packaged, and how it was transported to you. To live, we need to consume things, and yet we can choose to shop in a way that uses resources in the most sustainable way possible. This Earth Action will help you develop the necessary knowledge and skill.

EARTH ACTION
- Follow the Earth-friendly voting guidelines (see below) — QEEP — when shopping. Few products you buy will meet all the QEEP guidelines, but if you buy with the guidelines in mind and find products that meet as many as possible, you're on the right track.
1. Quality (Q): Choose products with the best quality, because they last longer.
2. Earth-friendliness (E): Consider the cost to the Earth. Is the product itself made from recycled materials? Can it be recycled? Is it locally made? Is it nontoxic? Is it biodegradable? Is it energy efficient?
3. Energy Star® rating (E): A product bearing the Energy Star® label has met strict government criteria for energy efficiency. Check the Energy Star® Website (www.energystar.gov) for further information and rebates.
4. Packaging (P): Examine the packaging. Did the manufacturer use as little as possible, or is there excess packaging? Is the packaging made from recyclable materials? Can you bring your own bag or container from home and buy in bulk or package-free?
- Look for addresses or toll-free phone numbers on the labels of the products you normally buy, and write or call those companies which you'd like to see make changes based on the QEEP guidelines.
  - Ask them to consider more Earth-friendly ways of making or packaging the product so that you are motivated to continue purchasing it. Companies really do pay attention, since they want to keep you as a customer.
  - If a company is producing an Earth-friendly product that meets many of the guidelines, consider writing or calling to thank them for their efforts.

MATERIALS
- The QEEP guidelines, phone, the determination to be an aware voter for the Earth.

TIME
- A few seconds more to read labels before purchasing; some time to write a few letters or make some calls.

RESOURCE SAVINGS

By voting for the Earth, you provide important feedback to manufacturers that it's important to be Earth-friendly in the ways they produce and package products. As a result, you lessen the demand for resources and landfill space. You win. And so does everyone else!

THINK BEFORE YOU BUY

CURBING YOUR SHOPPING IMPULSE

 Have you ever thought you needed something, but a few weeks after buying it, you wondered why you thought it was so important in the first place? Shopping has become a major pastime in the United States. And every time we buy something, we use the Earth's resources. This Earth Action will help you find fulfillment in ways the Earth can more easily sustain.

RESOURCE SAVINGS

You lessen the demand for resources to produce the item you decide you don't need after all. You are helping create a sustainable environment so that future generations will have the resources they need. You've thought globally and acted locally!

EARTH ACTION

- When you are about to purchase something, get in the habit of asking yourself, "Am I buying this item primarily to make myself feel good? If so, is there a nonresource-based alternative that will also give me a sense of satisfaction?" If you were going to purchase the item to help you feel good, consider redirecting the impulse. You might:
  - Offer service, make a gift, or donate the money you would have spent to an effort that is making a contribution to our world.
  - Cook a beautiful meal for your family or someone you care about.
  - Listen to music or take the time to relax and read a good book.

MATERIALS

- Awareness of the finite amount of resources our planet has to share with us.

TIME

- A moment to examine the reason for buying the item; more time for an alternate activity.

TOXIC SLEUTH
REDUCING TOXIC PRODUCTS IN THE HOME

Products we use to clean and fix up our homes, care for our yards and cars, and keep the bugs away, need to be used with care for our sake and the Earth's. Toxic products that are spread on the ground or washed down the drain can harm the soil and seep into underground streams finding their way into our drinking water. This Earth Action will help you identify harmful products and substitute them with Earth-friendly alternatives.

EARTH ACTION

• Make a list of products in your home that might be toxic.
   - Search all the places in your home where these products may be found: under sinks; in the kitchen closet and laundry room; in the workroom, shed, or garage.
   - If the words "danger," "warning," and/or "caution" appear on the label, it may be hazardous to you and your environment. If you have any questions, call your local or county environmental commission. You might also call the 800 number on the label, if there is one, and ask the company about its product.
• Find Earth-friendly products that will achieve the same desired results.
   - Call your local health food store, supermarket or home supply store to see whether they have Earth-friendly products that you could use to replace the toxic ones.
   - If your local stores do not routinely stock Earth-friendly products, ask them to carry these items.
• Use up what you have or call your town or city hall to find out where to properly dispose of the toxic products.
• If you must use toxic products be sure to store them safely where children and animals can't get to them.

MATERIALS
• Paper and pen, phone, Earth-friendly household products.

TIME
• Two to three hours.

RESOURCE SAVINGS

By making your home an Earth-friendly zone, you've protected your immediate quality of life. You are also protecting the quality of life for all of us!

A BREATH OF FRESH AIR

REDUCING THE AIR POLLUTION COMING FROM HOME PRODUCTS

WHY ACT? Poor air quality isn't just caused by pollutants from cars, boats and other gasoline-powered engines. Many household products (some that we use every day) contain chemicals that break down when exposed to sunlight and high temperature creating ground-level ozone, or what we call smog. Although ozone is the same chemical that is vital in the atmosphere to keep out ultraviolet radiation, when it is trapped at ground-level as smog, it can cause serious health consequences.

RESOURCE SAVINGS

You reduce outdoor air pollution and that benefits you and your community. You also reduce indoor air pollution and that benefits you and your family members.

EARTH ACTION

The goal is to reduce or stop using the following three categories of products, and to think before purchasing similar products.

1. Products that come in aerosol cans, especially personal care products like hair spray, deodorant, or air freshener. It is true that some harmful chemicals (like CFC's) have been banned from aerosols, but most aerosols still contribute to air pollution.

2. Paints, solvents, and cleaning products. These products also contribute to indoor air pollution. Look for low-solvent paints and less-toxic cleaning products.

3. Lighter fluids. To get those coals burning, use a charcoal chimney or an electric starter.

Remember to follow QEEP guidelines (p. 83) when replacing products, and to dispose of them properly.

NOTE: A product used every day is more harmful than a product used only once in a while.

MATERIALS

• Non-aerosol products, low-solvent paints, less toxic cleaning products, charcoal chimney, electric starter.

TIME

• A few moments to be more attentive, read labels and choose products carefully.

HOME SWEET HOME
BUYING NON-TOXIC FURNISHINGS AND BUILDING MATERIALS

 Our homes can shelter our bodies and soothe our souls so much better if we limit the use of building materials and home furnishings that contain toxic substances. This Earth Action will help you use products in your home that are healthier for the Earth and for your household.

EARTH ACTION
- When you buy home furnishings, steer in favor of untreated fabrics and natural fibers and materials.
- When planning a renovation or home repairs:
  - Use natural, unaltered building materials whenever possible.
  - Use low or zero VOC (Volatile Organic Compounds) paints such as non-petroleum-based latex paint which has fewer of the toxic solvents found in oil-based paint.

MATERIALS
- Home furnishings made with natural materials and fibers, natural, unaltered building materials, non-petroleum-based paints.

TIME
- A few minutes to do research when you are buying home furnishings or paint or planning a renovation.

RESOURCE SAVINGS

You've improved the quality of the air in your home by eliminating toxics, and you've created a demand for toxic-free home furnishings and building materials. You're a breath of fresh air yourself!

WHAT GOES AROUND CAME AROUND

BUYING RECYCLED PAPER PRODUCTS

If you're recycling paper, there's a good chance that within the next year someone will buy your discarded shopping lists, doodles, and computer printout rejects for a new generation of paper use. Recycling paper is important, but it's only half the solution. The other half is to buy recycled paper products. This Earth Action will show you how to be on the lookout for these items whenever you're buying paper products.

RESOURCE SAVINGS

You reduce the demand for trees and energy. Recycled paper requires 64% less energy and 58% less water, which results in 74% less air pollution and 35% less water pollution. It saves the demand for 17 trees per ton of paper made, and reduces the amount of solid waste going to the landfill. You've got the "write" stuff!

EARTH ACTION

- The next time you need to purchase paper products — notebook paper, tablets, sketch pads, greeting cards, toilet paper and so on — make sure you look for the recycled symbol. ♻
- Whenever possible, purchase paper that is labeled "post-consumer waste." That's the stuff people actually recycled, not just the trimmings from the paper mill floor.
- If your local stores don't sell recycled paper products, ask them to do so and tell them which items, specifically, you would like to have them carry.

MATERIALS

- Recycled paper products.

TIME

- Just a couple extra seconds to look for the recycling symbol and read labels.

RECYCLED

My Past Life As Junk Mail

100% RECYCLED POST-CONSUMER PAPER

VEGETABLE SOUP

BUYING ORGANIC PRODUCE

 Did you know it is more healthful for you and easier on the Earth to eat organic produce? Organic means the produce has been grown without toxic pesticides and has no dyes or wax coatings to preserve it. Even if you have to pay a little more, the extra money can be offset with savings from eating more vegetarian meals and taking other resource-saving actions. This Earth Action will help you to buy organic. Eat, be healthy, and support a healthier environment!

EARTH ACTION

- Call local food markets and health food stores to determine which ones sell organic vegetables and fruit, and begin shopping there.
- Read the food labels of packaged foods and beverages and try to purchase organically grown items whenever possible. Health food stores routinely stock these items, and many supermarkets are beginning to do so as well.

MATERIALS

- Phone book and phone, fresh organically grown food, a healthy appetite!

TIME

- A few minutes to locate sources for organic food; a few seconds to read labels.

RESOURCE SAVINGS

You help to keep our soil healthy and avoid the potential seepage of synthetic herbicides and pesticides into our groundwater. Here's to your health and that of our Earth!

NEAR AND DEAR
BUYING LOCAL PRODUCE AND DAIRY

 WHY ACT? Did you know the typical mouthful of American food travels over 1,000 miles from the farm to your dinner plate? Each mile has an environmental price in terms of the energy that is used. If you live on the East Coast, it will take three times the energy to truck a head of lettuce to you from the West Coast than it would to grow it at home. This Earth Action will help you reduce the demand for energy by cultivating an appetite for things that are locally grown. It will be easy, since locally grown produce is picked ripe and tastes far more delicious.

RESOURCE SAVINGS

You lessen the demand for the energy needed to transport food, and you improve air quality by contributing to reducing pollution. While helping to ensure future generations will have the fossil fuels they need, you also improve the quality of life of everyone in your household by providing them with fresher, tastier foods. Eat in good health!

EARTH ACTION

• Identify local sources where you can buy regionally-grown produce in season, such as farmers' markets, co-ops and produce stands, the health food store, and your supermarket.
  - Adjust your appetite and menu to eating more locally-grown produce. You'll know you're headed in the right direction by how fresh the food tastes!
  - In colder climates, substitute more produce that has a longer shelf life, such as root vegetables, during the winter months.
• Identify and patronize local dairies that produce any dairy products you use.
  - Ask your market to stock local dairy products if it doesn't already do so.
• Read food labels. Whenever you have a choice between a local food item versus one that comes from a distance, choose the product that traveled fewer miles.

NOTE: If you want to take this action a step further, consider joining a community garden or growing your own food.

MATERIALS
• Phone book and phone, locally grown food.

TIME
• An hour or two to identify local sources of produce and dairy products.

CHEW ON THIS FOR AWHILE

INCREASING MEATLESS MEALS

 WHY ACT? One of the most important actions you can take for the Earth is to broaden your diet and become less dependent on meat. Livestock produced by factory and rainforest farming are inefficient at converting grains and other resources into usable food. Beef requires 16 pounds of grain just to produce a pound of meat. This Earth Action will offer you alternative ideas for meals that use fewer resources.

EARTH ACTION

The goal is to increase the number of meatless meals over the next two weeks and commit to eating less meat afterward. Here's how to do it:

• Review your diet. See how much meat you eat, and look for opportunities to substitute vegetarian menus.
• Look through cookbooks for tasty vegetarian recipes. Then each time you enjoy a vegetarian meal, think about the savings to the Earth.
• Gather household members and discuss this action with them, encouraging them to join you in enjoying a vegetarian meal at home.
• Commit to eating at least one less meat meal a week.
• If you eat meat, consider choosing "free range" or "organic" varieties that will contribute to a healthy environment and greater health for you and your family.

NOTE: If you want to take this action even further, consider becoming a vegetarian.

MATERIALS

• Vegetables, grains, fruits, and nuts; a vegetarian cookbook or two.

TIME

• A few minutes to meet with household members; an hour to look through cookbooks and plan menus.

RESOURCE SAVINGS

Meat, egg and dairy production (including related feed production) account for 3/4 of all the water use in the U.S. What's more—a person with a red meat diet emits the global warming equivalent of approximately 5,000 pounds of CO_2 a year more than a person with a vegetarian diet.

SWAP PARTY
EXCHANGING ITEMS INSTEAD OF THROWING THEM AWAY

 WHY ACT? We need not consume the Earth's precious resources just to get some variety in our lives if variety is all we want. This Earth Action will provide you with a cost-free way to spice up your wardrobe or home that's fun and good for the planet.

RESOURCE SAVINGS

You lessen the demand for the resources needed to produce all the items you exchanged instead of bought. Using the resources of your community more efficiently and creatively is the way of the future. You're a pioneer!

EARTH ACTION
- Call friends or neighbors and ask them if they would like to participate in a "swap party." You might also wish to do this as an EcoTeam activity.
  - Consider exchanging things you might normally buy to add variety to your life, such as clothing, household items, or furniture.
  - Set a date and location for the exchange.
- Sort through your things and find items you no longer want that are still in good condition and would be suitable for the exchange.

NOTE: Consider having regular swap parties with friends.

MATERIALS
- Items you no longer need or want; items others no longer need that you want.

TIME
- An hour to find items no longer wanted that are suitable for exchange; 30 minutes to organize your swap party; about an hour to actually exchange the items; some more time if you choose to socialize.

LOAN ON ME

SHARING ITEMS WITH NEIGHBORS

 As you admire things belonging to others, does it ever occur to you that other people probably admire your stuff as well? Why not share each other's things on occasion to save both of you from having to buy your own? This system works especially well with tools and other items you don't need all the time. Here's an Earth Action that will show you how to have more of the things you want without using any more of the Earth's resources — or spending more money — to get them.

EARTH ACTION

- Become a loaner. As you think of things you've been wanting to purchase, consider ways you could borrow them instead from friends and colleagues. Then arrange to loan something in return that they could use. Be clear about how long the loan is for, and establish guidelines in the event the item is damaged.
- Speak to friends or EcoTeam members with similar interests about creating a lending "library" to share specific types of things, such as tools, garden implements, or sporting equipment, so each individual will not have to purchase his or her own items.
- If you have a neighborhood association, check to see if they have a lending program.

MATERIALS

- Something worth loaning; something worth borrowing.

TIME

- A few minutes to arrange a swap; some more time to establish a lending "library."

RESOURCE SAVINGS

You lessen the demand for the resources to produce the items you have chosen to share instead of buy. You save money and you have additional things to enjoy at no cost to our planet. Your savings are an investment in our Earth!

A GREEN GARDENER

REDUCING THE USE OF TOXIC PESTICIDES, HERBICIDES AND FERTILIZERS

WHY ACT? Whether you are growing gorgeous flowers or delicious tomatoes, consider doing this without using toxic pesticides, herbicides, and fertilizers. These chemicals can harm children, pets, and local wildlife and kill helpful insects such as ladybugs and green lacewings that keep real pests in check. Even when used sparingly, these chemicals can end up washing down storm drains, into streams and can eventually pollute the local water supply. This Earth Action will help you be a truly green gardener.

RESOURCE SAVINGS

By "greening" your garden you prevent fertilizers, toxic pesticides and herbicides from flowing into the water systems, all while making your garden a natural place for you, your family and neighbors to enjoy. You protect your family's health, the health of your neighbors and you also save the lives of local and beneficial wildlife.

EARTH ACTION

- To naturally strengthen the resistance of your plants to pests, build healthy soil. Use compost. Make your own compost, or purchase it. (See "Let It Rot" p. 10)
- Choose native plants that are naturally pest and drought resistant. Check with your local nursery or garden store.
- If unwelcome pests do appear, pull them off by hand or spray them with a diluted solution of phosphate-free soapy water. You can also pick off the affected part of the plant. Remember that insects are part of your garden's ecosystem. The occasional pest in your garden may also be a food source for beneficial insects, amphibians and birds. Learn to live with the occasional pest.

Note: If you must use fertilizers or pesticides, read the labels and follow all safety precautions. Use sparingly on a dry, windless day. Take leftover chemicals to a household hazardous waste collection site.

MATERIALS

- Compost, organic fertilizer, soap and water, pesticides as a last resort.

TIME

- A few hours to prepare your garden and some time to take care of it.

RELATING TO NATURE:
WHEN THE "GOTTA HAVE ITS" ATTACK, HEAD FOR THE GARDEN
GROWING YOUR OWN FOOD

We often buy things when what we are really searching for is a deeper sense of satisfaction. This Earth Action will help you experience a source of happiness that is regenerative to the Earth and you: planting a garden.

EARTH ACTION

- Plan a garden area for growing something you can eat. It can be as simple as lettuce and compact tomatoes growing in a hanging basket or large flower pot in the sun, or it can be a garden plot that sustains your entire household with produce.
  - Ask your local nursery for suitable varieties of plants. Remember to use your compost, if you have any. (See "Let It Rot" p. 10)
- If you already have a garden, consider planting a row or two for your local soup kitchen, homeless shelter, or other organization serving those in need.
  - If you have difficulty finding an organization near you, Second Harvest (www.secondharvest.org), a national clearinghouse for food banks, may be able to direct you to a local group.
- When the gotta-have-its attack, head for the garden and receive the Earth's natural abundance.

MATERIALS

- Garden plot; pots or hanging baskets; seeds or seedlings; phone.

TIME

- An hour or two to gather your seeds or seedlings and plant them; more time if you need to start your garden plot from scratch.

RESOURCE SAVINGS

You save all the energy that would have been needed to transport the food you have chosen to grow instead of buy. You are helping our Earth to prosper!

HEY, THIS IS FUN!

FARTHER DOWN THE PATH:

WHY ACT? Learning to become resource-efficient, a primary goal of this program, is an important part of living a more sustainable lifestyle. But to live sustainably involves more than just our impact on the environment. Once our material needs are adequately met, much of what we look for is non-material. Do you feel a greater need for community? Do you seek the sense of meaning and contribution that comes from being of service to others in need? Do you seek the serenity and joy from more time spent in the natural world? Do you wish to have more time to think, read and be with loved ones? Do you wish to spend more time cultivating inner renewal? If you're like many people, you probably answered yes to many of these questions. These human needs are in fact essential to sustaining a good quality of life. Many of us, however, are not meeting many of these basic non-material needs. This causes our lives to be out of balance, and we fall into increasingly more unsustainable lifestyle patterns, often substituting material resources to meet these non-material needs. This action will assist you in developing a more sustainable lifestyle.

EARTH ACTION

- The starting point is to ask yourself the question: What are the simple, non-material, pleasures that I wish to have more of in my life? Consider such things as more time with friends or family, a community service project, time in nature, etc.

  - List them, and next to each one indicate how much time it will take and how often you would like to partake of this simple pleasure.

  - Then ask yourself what activities you need to re-prioritize to do the things you just identified. So begins the adventure of self-negotiation about how you value your time. The awareness you get from this exercise will be enlightening. Are you willing to make the changes? If not, what gets in your way? Might you consider lessening time spent earning money, for time spent doing other things you find meaningful? What changes might this require of you in terms of your current material needs? Inevitably you will discover your core values and be able to make clearer choices for your life. A good resource to help you consider the economic/quality-of-life trade-offs is *Your Money or Your Life* by Vicki Robin and Joe Dominquez.

ACTION continued on next page

A SUSTAINABLE LIFESTYLE

- Based on these insights, create a plan for the next year allocating at least 20 hours a month for these special quality-of-life activities. What you will have created is your personal vision for living a more sustainable lifestyle. This is a great gift you give yourself. It's also a gift that benefits the Earth. The more fulfilled we become, the less we need to use the Earth's material resources to meet non-material needs.

NOTE: Invite all the members of your household to participate in this activity. This will allow for on-going positive reinforcement and support for your new sustainable lifestyle choices.

MATERIALS
Paper and pen.

TIME
An afternoon or evening to create your plan. Hours of new found time to enjoy the simple pleasures of life.

RESOURCE SAVINGS

Resources not used to meet non-material needs materially.

ACTION NOTES

YOU MAKE THE DIFFERENCE— ACTION LOG

Actions	Action Plan		Discussed with Household	Action Done	Points
Household by Household by Household	Day:	Time:	☐	☐	3
Cool Community	Day:	Time:	☐	☐	5
A Down-to-Earth Family	Day:	Time:	☐	☐	3
A Workable Idea	Day:	Time:	☐	☐	3
Citizenhood	Day:	Time:	☐	☐	4
Neighborhood Livability	Day:	Time:	☐	☐	4
Relating to the Planet: It's a Small World	Day:	Time:	☐	☐	2

STEP 6 · YOU MAKE THE DIFFERENCE

EMPOWERING OTHERS

Congratulations on your accomplishments! You may have challenged yourself and your teammates to go further than you imagined possible when you began. You can feel proud of your efforts. It may have also become obvious that to sustain the resources of our communities and planet, many of us will need to do our part. The final leg of your journey, then, is to reach out and encourage others to participate.

Many of us hold back from asking others to do something for fear of imposing. Our experience in working with the thousands of households who have gone through this program is that this fear is unwarranted. People are generally appreciative when someone invites them to participate in something as meaningful and community-building as an EcoTeam. Further, polls indicate that Americans are very much concerned about the environment and want to do the right thing. Witness the high recycling participation rates in most communities. With an explanation of the importance of living an environmentally sustainable lifestyle and encouragement, many people will take this next step.

We are in a time when Americans need to develop a new way of living to assure for our children and their children the planet's future sustainability. It is a time not unlike the American Revolution, when as an act of civic responsibility, neighbor reached out to neighbor for the benefit of all. People rose to the occasion and created a new country. We must once again create a new country: a sustainable America where Americans, for the sake of all, take responsibility to steward the resources they use. This is our generation's historic opportunity to create a legacy that will make our children proud. In this final section you will have a chance to reach out to your neighbors and invite them to be part of this great adventure. Your success is everyone's success. Good luck!

HOUSEHOLD BY HOUSEHOLD BY HOUSEHOLD
STARTING A NEW ECOTEAM

To have more sustainable communities, eventually we all need to live more sustainable lifestyles. This Earth Action will give you the chance to pass on what you have learned — person by person and household by household — until yours is a community of people committed to doing their part to ensure a better future for all of us.

EARTH ACTION

- Help create more household EcoTeams. The goal is to have every EcoTeam create at least one new team. Here's how:
  - Invite neighbors to the EcoTeam Introduction event sponsored by your team.
- The majority of people will be interested to attend an introduction event to learn more, if invited by their neighbors.
- Even if they are not interested in joining an EcoTeam right now, continue to be a good example to them. Watching you live an environmentally sustainable lifestyle may inspire them to participate in the future.

NOTE: For those who would like to work explicitly on the global warming issue, use this action to invite your friends and neighbors to participate in *Low Carbon Diet: A 30 Day Program to Lose 5,000 Pounds*. Using the same methodology as Green Living Handbook, this four meeting program helps households measure and reduce their carbon footprint by at least 5,000 pounds. See A Cool Community action on the next page for how to take *Low Carbon Diet* to your community.

MATERIALS
- A list of people to invite.

TIME
- A few minutes per person to invite them to your EcoTeam Introduction event.

RESOURCE SAVINGS

Each person you help to start on his or her journey can have similar savings to yours. In this way, you can double your savings for the Earth just by helping one extra person live a more sustainable lifestyle. Your sincere effort to reach out to others gives hope for our planet's future!

A COOL COMMUNITY

EMPOWER YOUR COMMUNITY TO GO ON A LOW CARBON DIET

 Imagine Americans coming together to do something about global warming. Imagine small and large groups gathering in our community centers, places of worship and town halls to speak their minds and hearts about the global crisis facing us, and taking action to turn it around. Imagine them being given the tools they need to reduce their own carbon footprints and the strategies to empower their communities to do the same. Imagine communities across the country engaged in a campaign, household by household, to reduce their carbon footprints 20% in three years. Now imagine that your community is part of it!

RESOURCE SAVINGS

You know the resources you saved in your own household. Imagine the same amount being saved by the many households in your community. Credit yourself 5,000 pounds for each household in your community that participates. You're a powerful agent of change in the world!

EARTH ACTION

- Visit Empowerment Institute's website at www.empowermentinstitute.net/lcd. Sign up for a free Cool Community Teletraining and learn how to launch a Cool Community Campaign, or just use resources on the website.
- Meet with community elected officials - mayor or town supervisor as well as your council member. Ask them to consider sponsoring a Cool Community Campaign. Share your experience of reducing your own carbon footprint, your vision for the campaign and willingness to contribute your time.

MATERIALS

- Computer, internet, and phone. Good community organizing skills if you are helping manage the campaign.

TIME

- If you participate directly, a long-term dedication of service to your community and planet.

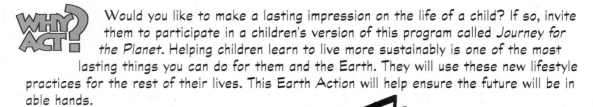

A DOWN-TO-EARTH FAMILY

HELPING CHILDREN LEARN TO LIVE MORE SUSTAINABLY

WHY ACT? Would you like to make a lasting impression on the life of a child? If so, invite them to participate in a children's version of this program called *Journey for the Planet*. Helping children learn to live more sustainably is one of the most lasting things you can do for them and the Earth. They will use these new lifestyle practices for the rest of their lives. This Earth Action will help ensure the future will be in able hands.

EARTH ACTION

- Tell your kids, or the children in your life, that you are doing your part to ensure the Earth will be healthy when they grow up. Then explain how they can do their part as well.
- Let them know they can go on a journey similar to yours that's just for kids.l
- If they are interested, you can get a copy of *Journey for the Planet* in your local bookstore or on-line at www.empowermentinstitute.net/journey.
- If you wish to take this further, consider bringing this program and its 26 lesson plan curriculum to your children's school or after school club. You can learn more about the "Cool School" program by visiting the same website.
- Set up a meeting with a teacher, youth program leader, principal, or superintendent.
- When you meet, talk about your experience of the *Green Living Handbook*, the results you achieved, and your vision for why you wish the school to participate in the Journey for the Planet program. Ask for his or her leadership to spearhead this for the school. Indicate your willingness to contribute your time to this endeavor as needed.
- It will take perseverance to get this in motion. Stay with it and continue your advocacy until you make it happen.

MATERIALS

- A copy of *Journey for the Planet*, phone.

TIME

- A few minutes to speak to the children in your life; some more time to establish a program in your local school or youth group.

RESOURCE SAVINGS

The journey the children take will help them use resources more sustainably for the rest of their lives. You are ensuring a better future for those who will be living in it!

A WORKABLE IDEA
TAKING ENVIRONMENTAL ACTIONS IN THE WORKPLACE

Now that you've put your own house in order, it's natural to want to practice your new, sustainable lifestyle all the time, including during work hours, assuming you work outside of the home. You may find that you are not always able to continue your Earth Actions at work, though, because there are no systems in place. Perhaps there is no recycling center or it's not as complete as it could be. Maybe carpools haven't been formed even though many of your coworkers live along the same route to work. Or maybe no bike rack has been installed where you and others could park your bikes. This Earth Action will help your workplace become more Earth-friendly so that you and others can live more sustainably through the whole day.

RESOURCE SAVINGS

You increase the amount of resource savings you are able to achieve every time a co-worker embarks on this journey. You're making a difference everywhere!

EARTH ACTION
- Go back through this book and choose an action or several actions you were unable to take at work because something needed is unavailable.
- Think through what would have to be done so that you could implement the action(s).
- Speak to your manager or employer, or if you are in charge, to your employees, and ask for their support. Volunteer your time to help bring this action(s) about.

MATERIALS
- Whatever materials are needed to change your workplace.

TIME
- 30 minutes to think about the changes needed at work; 15 minutes to speak with your manager or employer or, if you are the boss, with your employees; more time to implement the change.

CITIZENHOOD

ORGANIZING ENVIRONMENTAL PROJECTS IN YOUR COMMUNITY

Along your journey, there may have been actions you would have taken if only the support had existed in your community. You might have recycled certain items if your recycling center had accepted them. Maybe you would have bicycled to work if your community had safe bike lanes. And if public transportation were better, you might have been able to leave your car at home more often. This Earth Action will help you show your community how it can, in turn, help you and others to lead more Earth-friendly lives.

RESOURCE SAVINGS

By helping to make your community more Earth-friendly, you enable the resource savings to increase far beyond what one person can accomplish. You also raise the community's awareness during the process and a committed community can accomplish just about anything. You're a global citizen and a local hero!

EARTH ACTION

- Go back through this book and select one action you or your team were unable to take because what you needed wasn't available in your community.
- Carefully think through what would have to be done so that you could implement the action. Invite other team members to work with you.
- Call the mayor's office or the appropriate city or town official and ask for an appointment to share your concern and ideas.
- Volunteer your time to help the mayor or other official make your idea a reality. For example, volunteer to go to meetings to explain to others why you think your idea is important. Maybe you could head a committee to get it started or organize a group of volunteers whose work could offset part of the cost involved.

MATERIALS

- This book, a community need, persuasion skills, and a receptive city or town official.

TIME

- An hour to plan your meeting; half an hour to attend; more time to take the idea from there.

NEIGHBORHOOD LIVABILITY
STARTING A LIVABLE NEIGHBORHOOD TEAM

WHY ACT? Neighborhood-based teams that completed this program asked how they could use what they had learned to improve the overall livability of their neighborhood. This question spawned an obvious idea — extend the EcoTeam concept beyond the household to the neighborhood. The *Livable Neighborhood Program* helps neighbors create and act on their own visions of how they can transform their neighborhood into the kind of place they'd like it to be. This action helps you and your team take the work you have begun to the next level.

RESOURCE SAVINGS

A cleaner, safer, healthier, friendlier neighborhood that is kinder to the environment.

EARTH ACTION
• Go to Empowerment Institute's Website www.empowermentinstitute.net and click on *Livable Neighborhood Program*. Review the materials and print them out for your team.
• Present this idea to your team and encourage them to do the program.
• If they accept, order workbooks and start the program.

MATERIALS
• The *Livable Neighborhood Program* workbook can be ordered from the web site.

TIME
• A few minutes to view the website, 10-15 minutes to enroll your team.

RELATING TO THE PLANET: IT'S A SMALL WORLD

USING THE INTERNET TO INTEREST OTHERS IN STARTING AN ECOTEAM

 Why not bring together your interest in sustainable living and being a global citizen? Reach out through the mail or via the Internet to people you know or would like to know, and invite them to participate in an EcoTeam. This Earth Action will show you how.

EARTH ACTION
- Invite others to participate in either a Green Living or Low Carbon Diet EcoTeam via e-mail.
  - E-mail and have them view Empowerment Institute's Website at www.empowermentinstitute.net.

MATERIALS
- Friends in another part of this country; a computer, modem, and access to the Internet; online friends.

TIME
- 15 minutes to write a friend or communicate with someone about becoming an EcoTeam member.

RESOURCE SAVINGS

You multiply your own resource savings by all the other people around the world you have encouraged to participate in EI's sustainable lifestyle program. You are fully exercising your power as a global citizen!

ACTION NOTES

SUSTAINABLE LIFESTYLE ASSESSMENT

SUSTAINABLE LIFESTYLE ASSESSMENT GUIDELINES

1. The Sustainable Lifestyle Assessment will help you become more aware of the environmental impact of your daily lifestyle choices and determine which actions you wish to take in the program.

2. To get the most value from your participation in this program, please fill this out thoughtfully. The most accurate reflection of your household's accomplishments can be assured if the same person fills in both the "before" and "after" sections of the assessment.

3. Before each topic meeting, read the chapter in the handbook and fill out the "before" column of that section of the Sustainable Lifestyle Assessment. Make your action plan by checking the "will do action", and then transfer it to the Action Log in the beginning of each chapter.

4. To keep track of your accomplishments, after you have done each action, check it off on your Action Log and fill in the "after program" column of the Sustainable Lifestyle Assessment.

ACTIONS	BEFORE PROGRAM	WILL DO ACTION	AFTER PROGRAM

1. BACK BY POPULAR DEMAND - *Recycling*

Which of these items do you recycle?

	BEFORE PROGRAM	WILL DO ACTION	AFTER PROGRAM
Newspaper	❑	❑	❑ Newspaper
Paper	❑	❑	❑ Paper
Junk Mail	❑	❑	❑ Junk Mail
Corrugated cardboard	❑	❑	❑ Corrugated cardboard
Gray cardboard	❑	❑	❑ Gray cardboard
Metal	❑	❑	❑ Metal
Glass	❑	❑	❑ Glass
Plastic	❑	❑	❑ Plastic
Motor Oil	❑	❑	❑ Motor Oil
Tires	❑	❑	❑ Tires
Household Batteries	❑	❑	❑ Household Batteries
Car Batteries	❑	❑	❑ Car Batteries
Other (specify) _____	❑	❑	❑ Other (specify) _____

Using the above items as a guide, what percent of recyclable materials do you actually recycle?

	N/A	0	20%	40%	60%	80%	100%	WILL DO ACTION	0	20%	40%	60%	80%	100%
	❑	❑	❑	❑	❑	❑	❑	❑	❑	❑	❑	❑	❑	❑

2. BAG BAGS - *Re-using bags*

How often do you use reusable, cloth bags or a backpack when you shop?

	N/A	0	20%	40%	60%	80%	100%	WILL DO ACTION	0	20%	40%	60%	80%	100%
	❑	❑	❑	❑	❑	❑	❑	❑	❑	❑	❑	❑	❑	❑

3. BRING YOUR OWN - *Reusing containers*

How often do you reuse containers for:

Bulk food purchases?

	N/A	0	20%	40%	60%	80%	100%	WILL DO ACTION	0	20%	40%	60%	80%	100%
	❑	❑	❑	❑	❑	❑	❑	❑	❑	❑	❑	❑	❑	❑

Restaurant take-out?

	N/A	0	20%	40%	60%	80%	100%	WILL DO ACTION	0	20%	40%	60%	80%	100%
	❑	❑	❑	❑	❑	❑	❑	❑	❑	❑	❑	❑	❑	❑

Restaurant leftovers?

	N/A	0	20%	40%	60%	80%	100%	WILL DO ACTION	0	20%	40%	60%	80%	100%
	❑	❑	❑	❑	❑	❑	❑	❑	❑	❑	❑	❑	❑	❑

ACTIONS	BEFORE PROGRAM	WILL DO ACTION	AFTER PROGRAM

4. TWO SIDES ARE BETTER THAN ONE - *Using paper on both sides before recycling*

How often do you use both sides of a piece of paper before recycling?

BEFORE: N/A 0 20% 40% 60% 80% 100% ❑❑❑ ❑ ❑ ❑ ❑   WILL DO: ❑   AFTER: 0 20% 40% 60% 80% 100% ❑❑ ❑ ❑ ❑ ❑

How often do you re-use envelopes?

BEFORE: N/A 0 20% 40% 60% 80% 100% ❑❑❑ ❑ ❑ ❑ ❑   WILL DO: ❑   AFTER: 0 20% 40% 60% 80% 100% ❑❑ ❑ ❑ ❑ ❑

5. JUNK MAIL DIET - *Reducing junk mail*

Have you taken steps to reduce junk mail in the last six months?

BEFORE: ❑ Yes ❑ No   WILL DO: ❑   AFTER: ❑ Yes ❑ No

6. LET IT ROT - *Composting*

Do you compost food waste?

BEFORE: ❑ Yes ❑ No   WILL DO: ❑   AFTER: ❑ Yes ❑ No

Do you compost yard waste?

BEFORE: ❑ Yes ❑ No   WILL DO: ❑   AFTER: ❑ Yes ❑ No

7. WIPE SWIPE - *Using cloth instead of paper towels*

How often do you use cloth instead of paper for:

Napkins?

BEFORE: N/A 0 20% 40% 60% 80% 100% ❑❑❑ ❑ ❑ ❑ ❑   WILL DO: ❑   AFTER: 0 20% 40% 60% 80% 100% ❑❑ ❑ ❑ ❑ ❑

Towels for cleanup?

BEFORE: N/A 0 20% 40% 60% 80% 100% ❑❑❑ ❑ ❑ ❑ ❑   WILL DO: ❑   AFTER: 0 20% 40% 60% 80% 100% ❑❑ ❑ ❑ ❑ ❑

Handkerchiefs?

BEFORE: N/A 0 20% 40% 60% 80% 100% ❑❑❑ ❑ ❑ ❑ ❑   WILL DO: ❑   AFTER: 0 20% 40% 60% 80% 100% ❑❑ ❑ ❑ ❑ ❑

8. A-MEND - *Repairing items instead of throwing them away*

Since your EcoTeam began have you repaired any items that you previously would have sent to the landfill?

WILL DO: ❑   AFTER: ❑ Yes ❑ No

List any appliances, furniture or heavy items (over 35 lbs.) _____

ACTIONS	BEFORE PROGRAM	WILL DO ACTION	AFTER PROGRAM

9. TRASH OR TREASURE - *Donating or selling used items*

Since your EcoTeam formed have you given away or sold any items that you previously would have sent to the landfill?

☐   ☐ Yes ☐ No

List any appliances, furniture or heavy items (over 35 lbs.): _____

10. CELEBRATE WITH THE EARTH IN MIND - *Using reusable party-products*

How often do you use reusable items instead of disposables at social events? (Plates, Cups, Napkins, Tablecloths, Silverware, Giftwrap)

N/A 0 20% 40% 60% 80% 100%
☐ ☐ ☐ ☐ ☐ ☐ ☐

☐

0 20% 40% 60% 80% 100%
☐ ☐ ☐ ☐ ☐ ☐

11. POOP SCOOP - *Cleaning up after your dog*

If you have a dog, do you scoop the poop and:

Flush it down your toilet?

☐ Yes ☐ No   ☐   ☐ Yes ☐ No

Bury it in a hole in your yard?

☐ Yes ☐ No   ☐   ☐ Yes ☐ No

12. CUT IT HIGH AND LET IT LIE - *Mulching grass*

MULCH! MULCH!

If you have a lawn, do you leave the clippings on the ground as mulch after you mow it?

☐ Yes ☐ No   ☐   ☐ Yes ☐ No

13. FARTHER DOWN THE PATH - *Creating a zero garbage household*

Do you have a plan for becoming a zero garbage household?

☐ Yes ☐ No   ☐   ☐ Yes ☐ No

ACTIONS

BEFORE PROGRAM

WILL DO ACTION

AFTER PROGRAM

1. AQUACOP -
Finding water leaks in your home

Have you looked for and fixed any indoor water leaks since your EcoTeam began?

❑ Yes ❑ No

If so, how many leaks did you find? How many have you fixed?

Fast = A trickle
Medium = More than one drop per second
Slow = One drop every four seconds

Found
# of Fast leaks _____
# of Medium leaks _____
# of Slow leaks _____
# of Toilet leaks _____

❑

Fixed
# of Fast leaks _____
# of Medium leaks _____
# of Slow leaks _____
# of Toilet leaks _____

ACTIONS	BEFORE PROGRAM	WILL DO ACTION	AFTER PROGRAM

2. TANKS A LOT -
Reducing water used for toilet flushing

How many toilets are there in your house?

How many are low-flow?

How many have a toilet dam?

How many have plastic jugs?

	BEFORE	WILL DO	AFTER
# Toilets total	____		# Toilets total ____
# Low-flow	____	☐	# Low-flow ____
# Toilet Dams	____	☐	# Toilet Dams ____
# Plastic Jugs	____	☐	# Plastic Jugs ____

OK, A LITTLE TO THE LEFT!

3. GO WITH THE FLOW -
Reducing the number of toilet flushes

On average, how many times a day is a toilet flushed in your home?

Flushes ____ ☐ # Flushes ____

WOW!

HEY! LET IT MELLOW!

4. AQUATECH -
Installing water saving devices

How many showers in your home have low-flow showerheads?

How many do not?

Low-flow showers___ ☐ # Low-flow showers___

Not low-flow showers ___ # Not low-flow showers ___

How many faucets in your home have aerators?

How many do not?

Faucets w/ aerators____ ☐ # Faucets w/ aerators___

Faucets without _____ # Faucets without ___

| ACTIONS | BEFORE PROGRAM | WILL DO ACTION | AFTER PROGRAM |

5. AM I CLEAN YET? -
Reducing use of shower and bath water

The length of your shower is the total minutes the water is running. Put a clock or watch, a pen and a sheet of paper with each participating household member's name in the bathroom. Ask each person to time their average shower and record the result. Ask each person how many showers and baths they take each week and fill in the chart:

Shower minutes per week

Household Member	minutes		# per wk	
1.		×		=
2.		×		=
3.		×		=
4.		×		=
5.		×		=
6.		×		=
Household Total....				

☐

Shower minutes per week

Household Member	minutes		# per wk	
1.		×		=
2.		×		=
3.		×		=
4.		×		=
5.		×		=
6.		×		=
Household Total....				

Baths per week

Household Member	1/2 full	full
1.		
2.		
3.		
4.		
5.		
6.		
Household Total....		

☐

Baths per week

Household Member	1/2 full	full
1.		
2.		
3.		
4.		
5.		
6.		
Household Total....		

6. SCRUB-A-DUB RUB -
Reducing water used in personal care

What percent of the time do you turn off the water while shaving, brushing your teeth and washing your hands or face?

N/A 0 20% 40% 60% 80% 100%
☐ ☐ ☐ ☐ ☐ ☐ ☐   ☐   0 20% 40% 60% 80% 100%
☐ ☐ ☐ ☐ ☐ ☐

7. SCRUB-A-DUB TUB -
Reducing water used to wash dishes

What is your average number of dishwasher loads per week?

dishwasher loads ____   ☐   # dishwasher loads ____

What percent of the time is your dishwasher full when it's run?

N/A 0 20% 40% 60% 80% 100%
☐ ☐ ☐ ☐ ☐ ☐ ☐   ☐   0 20% 40% 60% 80% 100%
☐ ☐ ☐ ☐ ☐ ☐

How many times per week do you wash dishes by hand?

# of times
we handwash dishes_____   ☐   # of times
we handwash dishes_____

When washing dishes by hand, what percent of the time do you leave the water running?

N/A 0 20% 40% 60% 80% 100%
☐ ☐ ☐ ☐ ☐ ☐ ☐   ☐   0 20% 40% 60% 80% 100%
☐ ☐ ☐ ☐ ☐ ☐

ACTIONS	BEFORE PROGRAM	WILL DO ACTION	AFTER PROGRAM

8. ALL BOTTLED UP -
Drinking refrigerated water
What percent of the time do household members drink tap water from a refrigerated container instead of running the tap until the water gets cold?

BEFORE PROGRAM: N/A ☐ 0 ☐ 20% ☐ 40% ☐ 60% ☐ 80% ☐ 100% ☐

WILL DO ACTION: ☐

AFTER PROGRAM: 0 ☐ 20% ☐ 40% ☐ 60% ☐ 80% ☐ 100% ☐

9. HOLD THE SALT -
Minimizing salt used by water softeners
If you use a water softener, is it adjusted for the most efficient salt usage?

BEFORE: ☐ Yes ☐ No   WILL DO: ☐   AFTER: ☐ Yes ☐ No

10. PURE AND SIMPLE -
Checking your water purity
Have you tested your water for purity?

BEFORE: ☐ Yes ☐ No   WILL DO: ☐   AFTER: ☐ Yes ☐ No

11. NO PHOS-FOR-US -
Earth-friendly car washing
Do you use a biodegradable phosphate-free soap when washing your car?

BEFORE: ☐ Yes ☐ No   WILL DO: ☐   AFTER: ☐ Yes ☐ No

Do you wash your car on grass or gravel to avoid run-off into the sewer system?

BEFORE: ☐ Yes ☐ No   WILL DO: ☐   AFTER: ☐ Yes ☐ No

If you use a hose to wash your car, does it have an on/off switch or nozzle?

BEFORE: ☐ Yes ☐ No   WILL DO: ☐   AFTER: ☐ Yes ☐ No

ACTIONS	BEFORE PROGRAM	WILL DO ACTION	AFTER PROGRAM

12. WHERE MY WATER COMES FROM- *Getting acquainted with your watershed.*

Do you know what watershed your water comes from?

❑ Yes ❑ No   ❑   ❑ Yes ❑ No

Are you aware of any threats to the water quality of your watershed?

❑ Yes ❑ No   ❑   ❑ Yes ❑ No

Do you dispose of toxic fluids properly?

❑ Yes ❑ No   ❑   ❑ Yes ❑ No

13. A NO-RAINER - *Reducing the amount of water going into the sewer system*

If you have gutters on your house, are they free of debris?

❑ Yes ❑ No   ❑   ❑ Yes ❑ No

Do they discharge the rain water so as to minimize the amount going into the sewer system? For example, is water directed to be soaked up in your yard or stored in a cistern?

❑ Yes ❑ No   ❑   ❑ Yes ❑ No

14. THE LAWN RANGER - *Reducing water used for your lawn*

How much do you water per week using a garden hose or sprinkler?

Minutes per week_____   ❑   Minutes per week_____

How many months of the year do you water?

Months per year_____   ❑   Months per year_____

What percent of the time is your lawn and/or garden watered early in the morning or late in the day to minimize evaporation?

N/A	0	20%	40%	60%	80%	100%		0	20%	40%	60%	80%	100%
❑	❑	❑	❑	❑	❑	❑	❑	❑	❑	❑	❑	❑	❑

ACTIONS	BEFORE PROGRAM	WILL DO ACTION	AFTER PROGRAM

15. A NATURAL LAWN –
Reducing the use of weed killers and fertilizers

If you fertilize, do you use an organic or slow release fertilizer?	❑ Yes ❑ No	❑	❑ Yes ❑ No
Do you overseed your lawn to crowd out weeds?	❑ Yes ❑ No	❑	❑ Yes ❑ No
Do you hand pull weeds to avoid using chemical weed killers?	❑ Yes ❑ No	❑	❑ Yes ❑ No

16. A MASTER WATERER –
Reducing water used for gardening

How much do you water per week using a garden hose or sprinkler?	Minutes per week_____	❑	Minutes per week_____
How many months of the year do you water?	Months per year_____	❑	Months per year_____
Do you use drip irrigation?	❑ Yes ❑ No	❑	❑ Yes ❑ No
Do you use grey water?	❑ Yes ❑ No	❑	❑ Yes ❑ No
Do any of your outdoor faucets or hoses leak? ❑ Yes ❑ No How many?	# outdoor leaks _____	❑	# outdoor leaks _____
How much of your yard is planted with native, or drought-tolerant plants that survive on native rainfall?	N/A 0 20% 40% 60% 80% 100% ❑ ❑ ❑ ❑ ❑ ❑ ❑	❑	0 20% 40% 60% 80% 100% ❑ ❑ ❑ ❑ ❑ ❑

ACTIONS	BEFORE PROGRAM	WILL DO ACTION	AFTER PROGRAM

17. DOWN BY THE RIVER - *Creating a sustainable streamside ecosystem*

Do you live near a stream?
Yes ❑ No ❑

Has your stream been invaded by non-native plants or a single kind of plant (monoculture)?	❑ Yes ❑ No	❑	❑ Yes ❑ No
Have you taken steps to restore native plants?	❑ Yes ❑ No	❑	❑ Yes ❑ No
If your streamside is eroding, have you taken steps to repair it?	❑ Yes ❑ No	❑	❑ Yes ❑ No

18. FARTHER DOWN THE PATH - *Sustainable landscaping*

What percent of your yard requires mowing?	N/A 0 20% 40% 60% 80% 100% ❑ ❑ ❑ ❑ ❑ ❑ ❑	❑	0 20% 40% 60% 80% 100% ❑ ❑ ❑ ❑ ❑ ❑
Have you developed a landscaping plan that minimizes the water needed for maintenance?	❑ Yes ❑ No	❑	❑ Yes ❑ No

	BEFORE PROGRAM							WILL DO ACTION	AFTER PROGRAM					

If you use alternative energy sources, what percent of your total energy is supplied by these means:

	N/A	0	20%	40%	60%	80%	100%		0	20%	40%	60%	80%	100%
Solar - generated at home?	☐	☐	☐	☐	☐	☐	☐	☐	☐	☐	☐	☐	☐	☐
Wind - generated at home?	☐	☐	☐	☐	☐	☐	☐	☐	☐	☐	☐	☐	☐	☐
"Green" energy - purchased from your utility company?	☐	☐	☐	☐	☐	☐	☐	☐	☐	☐	☐	☐	☐	☐
other? - Describe:	☐	☐	☐	☐	☐	☐	☐	☐	☐	☐	☐	☐	☐	☐

_____

_____

ACTIONS	BEFORE PROGRAM	WILL DO ACTION	AFTER PROGRAM

1. A BRIGHT IDEA- *Turning off unused lights and appliances*

When you aren't using them, what percent of the time do you turn off:

Lights?

	N/A	0	20%	40%	60%	80%	100%			0	20%	40%	60%	80%	100%
Lights?	❑	❑	❑	❑	❑	❑	❑	❑		❑	❑	❑	❑	❑	❑
Appliances?	❑	❑	❑	❑	❑	❑	❑	❑		❑	❑	❑	❑	❑	❑

Do you have timers on any of your lights? ❑ Yes ❑ No

If so, how many?

timers _____   ❑   # timers _____

2. PLUG YOUR ELECTRICITY LEAKS - *Turning appliances off when not in use*

What percent of the time do you completely turn off appliances - such as TVs, stereos and video players - by unplugging them or switching them off with a switched cord or power strip?

	N/A	0	20%	40%	60%	80%	100%			0	20%	40%	60%	80%	100%
	❑	❑	❑	❑	❑	❑	❑	❑		❑	❑	❑	❑	❑	❑

How many of your electronic appliances - such as stereo, TV, microwave, dryer, air conditioner or dishwasher - carry an Energy Star® rating?

# of appliances w/ Energy Star® rating ___   ❑   # of appliances w/ Energy Star® rating ___

3. HOW GREEN IS YOUR COMPUTER? - *Energy-efficient computer use*

If you have a computer does the monitor carry the Energy Star® rating?

❑Yes ❑No ❑Don't Know   ❑   ❑Yes ❑No ❑Don't Know

The Energy Star® rating will be a priority in the next computer I/we purchase.

❑   ❑ Yes ❑ No

Have you activated the **sleep, suspend** or **energy saver** feature on your computer monitor?

❑ Yes ❑ No   ❑   ❑ Yes ❑ No

Do you shut off your computers when they're not in use for two hours or more?

❑ Yes ❑ No   ❑   ❑ Yes ❑ No

ACTIONS	BEFORE PROGRAM	WILL DO ACTION	AFTER PROGRAM

4. LIGHT OF YOUR LIFE-
Installing energy-efficient lighting

How many light bulbs in your house or yard do you use for more than two consecutive hours a day, on average?

heavy use bulbs _____   ☐   # heavy use bulbs _____

How many of these light bulbs are compact fluorescent?

compact fluorescents _____   ☐   # compact fluorescents _____

Do you have a plan for increasing the number of compact fluorescents in your home and yard?

☐ Yes ☐ No   ☐   ☐ Yes ☐ No

If so, how many new compact fluorescents did/will you install this year?

compact fluorescents _____   ☐   # compact fluorescents _____

5. WEAR IT AGAIN SAM -
Washing and drying clothes efficiently

What percent of the time do household members wear clothes until they actually need to be washed, instead of washing them after one or two uses whether or not they need it?

WELL, IT SURE IS NICE TO GET OUTSIDE!
YEAH, THE SUN FEELS GOOD!

N/A 0 20% 40% 60% 80% 100%
☐ ☐ ☐ ☐ ☐ ☐ ☐   ☐   0 20% 40% 60% 80% 100%
☐ ☐ ☐ ☐ ☐ ☐

What percent of the time do you use cold water to wash and rinse your clothes?

Wash:
N/A 0 20% 40% 60% 80% 100%
☐ ☐ ☐ ☐ ☐ ☐ ☐   ☐   Wash:
0 20% 40% 60% 80% 100%
☐ ☐ ☐ ☐ ☐ ☐

Rinse:
N/A 0 20% 40% 60% 80% 100%
☐ ☐ ☐ ☐ ☐ ☐ ☐   ☐   Rinse:
0 20% 40% 60% 80% 100%
☐ ☐ ☐ ☐ ☐ ☐

On average, how many washing machine loads of laundry does your household do per week?

loads/week_____   ☐   loads/week_____

Of these loads, how many are typically full loads?

full loads/week_____   ☐   **full** loads/week_____

What percent of the time does your household use a clothesline or drying rack instead of a dryer?

N/A 0 20% 40% 60% 80% 100%
☐ ☐ ☐ ☐ ☐ ☐ ☐   ☐   0 20% 40% 60% 80% 100%
☐ ☐ ☐ ☐ ☐ ☐

ACTIONS	BEFORE PROGRAM	WILL DO ACTION	AFTER PROGRAM

6. MEET YOUR WATER HEATER- *Making your water heater more efficient*

What is the main fuel that heats your home's water?

BEFORE PROGRAM	WILL DO ACTION	AFTER PROGRAM
❑ 1. Electricity	❑	❑ 1. Electricity
❑ 2. Natural gas		❑ 2. Natural gas
❑ 3. Oil		❑ 3. Oil
❑ 4. Propane ❑ 5. Solar		❑ 4. Propane ❑ 5. Solar

What is the temperature setting on your water heater?

BEFORE PROGRAM	WILL DO ACTION	AFTER PROGRAM
_____ Degrees or ❑ Low ❑ Med ❑ High	❑	_____ Degrees or ❑ Low ❑ Med ❑ High

If your water heater has a timer, do you turn it off at night or when you're away for more than a day?

BEFORE PROGRAM	WILL DO ACTION	AFTER PROGRAM
❑ Yes ❑ No	❑	❑ Yes ❑ No

Has your water heater been tuned up/replaced within the last two years?

BEFORE PROGRAM	WILL DO ACTION	AFTER PROGRAM
❑ Tuned Up	❑	❑ Tuned Up
❑ Replaced	❑	❑ Replaced

Do you turn the water heater to a lower setting midday, at night, or when you go away for a week or more?

BEFORE PROGRAM	WILL DO ACTION	AFTER PROGRAM
❑ Midday	❑	❑ Midday
❑ Night	❑	❑ Night
❑ Away	❑	❑ Away

Does your water heater have adequate internal insulation or an insulating blanket?

BEFORE PROGRAM	WILL DO ACTION	AFTER PROGRAM
❑ Yes ❑ No	❑	❑ Yes ❑ No

Are your hot water pipes insulated?

BEFORE PROGRAM	WILL DO ACTION	AFTER PROGRAM
❑ Yes ❑ No	❑	❑ Yes ❑ No

7. FRIDGE PHYSICAL- *Making your refrigerator more efficient*

How many refrigerators do you currently use?

If you have and use more than one refrigerator, answer the following questions for your primary refrigerator:

BEFORE PROGRAM	AFTER PROGRAM
# refrigerators _____	# refrigerators _____

ZIP!

oo! THAT TICKLES!

What year was your refrigerator purchased new?

BEFORE PROGRAM	WILL DO ACTION	AFTER PROGRAM
_____ Yr. purchased new	❑	_____ Yr. purchased new (If you purchased a new one since being on your EcoTeam)

ACTIONS	BEFORE PROGRAM	WILL DO ACTION	AFTER PROGRAM
Does it carry the Energy Star® rating?	☐ Yes ☐ No ☐ Don't Know	☐	☐ Yes ☐ No ☐ Don't Know
Have you checked the door seal in the past year?	☐ Yes ☐ No	☐	☐ Yes ☐ No
Have you changed the door seal in the past year?	☐ Yes ☐ No	☐	☐ Yes ☐ No
Have you vacuumed the condenser coils in the past year?	☐ Yes ☐ No	☐	☐ Yes ☐ No
What temperature is it set for?	_____ Degrees or ☐ Low ☐ Med ☐ High	☐	_____ Degrees or ☐ Low ☐ Med ☐ High

8. BETTER A SWEATER-
Turning down the thermostat

ACTIONS	BEFORE PROGRAM	WILL DO ACTION	AFTER PROGRAM
Do you have a thermostat for your heating system?	☐ Yes ☐ No	☐	☐ Yes ☐ No
Can you program it?	☐ Yes ☐ No	☐	☐ Yes ☐ No
In cold weather, **at what temperature** do you set your thermostat?	When people are home___ When no one is home___ When sleeping___	☐	When people are home___ When no one is home___ When sleeping___

9. FURNACE FLING-
Making your furnace more efficient

ACTIONS	BEFORE PROGRAM	WILL DO ACTION	AFTER PROGRAM
What is the main fuel that heats your home?	☐ 1. Electricity ☐ 2. Natural gas ☐ 3. Oil ☐ 4. Propane ☐ 5. Solar		
If you have a furnace: What year was your furnace purchased new?	_____Yr. purchased new	☐	_____Yr. purchased new (If you purchased a new one since being on your EcoTeam)
What does it burn?	☐ 1. Natural gas ☐ 2. Oil ☐ 3. Propane		☐ 1. Natural gas ☐ 2. Oil ☐ 3. Propane
Has it been tuned up in the last two years?	☐ Yes ☐ No	☐	☐ Yes ☐ No
Are your heating ducts sealed?	☐ Yes ☐ No	☐	☐ Yes ☐ No
Are your heating ducts insulated?	☐ Yes ☐ No	☐	☐ Yes ☐ No

ACTIONS	BEFORE PROGRAM	WILL DO ACTION	AFTER PROGRAM

10. PUTTING ON AIRS- *Insulating windows and doors*

How many exterior windows and glass doors are in your home?

# windows/doors _____	❑	# windows/doors _____

How many of these are well-insulated against energy loss (double panes, storm windows, insulated drapes)?

# well insulated _____	❑	# well insulated _____

11. CHILL OUT- *Adding weatherstripping and caulking; Getting an energy audit*

How many of your windows and exterior doors have adequate weather stripping, putty, caulking, and "sweeps"(for doors)?

# doors and windows weather-stripped_____	❑	# doors and windows weather-stripped_____

If your electrical outlets need insulators, how many have you insulated?

# electrical outlets insulated _____	❑	# electrical outlets insulated _____

Have you scheduled an energy audit in your home?

❑ Yes ❑ No	❑	❑ Yes ❑ No

Have you had an energy audit in your home?

❑ Yes ❑ No	❑	❑ Yes ❑ No

Schedule an Energy Audit:

An energy audit is an analysis of your home's energy efficiency.

1. Start by calling your local utility to request an energy audit for your home. In some communities, government sponsored or non-profit organizations also provide this service at no, or low cost.

2. Your auditor can estimate the payback time for installing insulation or a new furnace (if needed).

3. Some energy auditors also provide applications for low-interest loans to make your home more energy-efficient.

ACTIONS

	BEFORE PROGRAM	WILL DO ACTION	AFTER PROGRAM

When you have your Energy meeting, you may look for air leaks in your house. Fill in this section at that time:

Are there obvious air leaks in your home (under doors, around windows, in cracks, etc.) that cause you to lose heated or cooled air?

BEFORE PROGRAM: ❑ Yes ❑ No   WILL DO ACTION: ❑   AFTER PROGRAM: ❑ Yes ❑ No

Have you checked for small air leaks using, for example, a candle or incense to show the leaks?

BEFORE PROGRAM: ❑ Yes ❑ No   WILL DO ACTION: ❑   AFTER PROGRAM: ❑ Yes ❑ No

If so, what percent of the small air leaks have you plugged in your home?

BEFORE PROGRAM: N/A ❑ 0 ❑ 20% ❑ 40% ❑ 60% ❑ 80% ❑ 100% ❑
WILL DO ACTION: ❑
AFTER PROGRAM: 0 ❑ 20% ❑ 40% ❑ 60% ❑ 80% ❑ 100% ❑

12. CHILL IN- *Cooling your house more efficiently*

In hot weather, if you have windows in the direct sun, what percent of the time do you keep shades or curtains drawn during the heat of the day?

BEFORE PROGRAM: N/A ❑ 0 ❑ 20% ❑ 40% ❑ 60% ❑ 80% ❑ 100% ❑
WILL DO ACTION: ❑
AFTER PROGRAM: 0 ❑ 20% ❑ 40% ❑ 60% ❑ 80% ❑ 100% ❑

Could your home be more fully shaded in the summer if additional trees were planted?
Yes ❑ No ❑

How many shade trees have you planted since starting your EcoTeam?

WILL DO ACTION: ❑   AFTER PROGRAM: # trees planted_____

If you do not own or use an air conditioner, please skip to question #13

ACTIONS	BEFORE PROGRAM	WILL DO ACTION	AFTER PROGRAM
Does your air conditioner unit or system have the Energy Star® rating?	❑Yes ❑No ❑Don't Know	❑	❑Yes ❑No ❑Don't Know
Is your air conditioner unit or system in the shade during the summer?	❑ Yes ❑ No	❑	❑ Yes ❑ No
Do you clean or replace the filter when needed (could be as often as monthly during high use times)?	❑ Yes ❑ No	❑	❑ Yes ❑ No
Do you clean the entire unit/system once a year?	❑ Yes ❑ No	❑	❑ Yes ❑ No
Do you turn your air conditioner to a warmer setting if you are gone for more than one hour?	❑ Yes ❑ No	❑	❑ Yes ❑ No
If you have central A/C, has it been serviced within three years?	❑ Yes ❑ No	❑	❑ Yes ❑ No
What temperature do you usually set the thermostat at?	_____ Degrees or ❑ coolest ❑ cooler ❑ cool	❑	_____ Degrees or ❑ coolest ❑ cooler ❑ cool
If you have single A/C units, do you have timers for them?	❑ Yes ❑ No	❑	❑ Yes ❑ No

13. FANS ARE COOL -
Using fans to cool your home

ACTIONS	BEFORE PROGRAM	WILL DO ACTION	AFTER PROGRAM
Do you use fans to circulate air through your living space?	❑ Yes ❑ No	❑	❑ Yes ❑ No
Do you have a whole-house fan to move the heat out of the top of your house?	❑ Yes ❑ No	❑	❑ Yes ❑ No

ACTIONS	BEFORE PROGRAM	WILL DO ACTION	AFTER PROGRAM

14. WHAT YOU SEE IS WHAT YOU BREATHE -
Preventing air pollution.

What percent of the time do you refuel gas powered equipment (car, boat, lawn mower) during cooler hours?

BEFORE PROGRAM: N/A ☐ 0 ☐ 20% ☐ 40% ☐ 60% ☐ 80% ☐ 100% ☐
WILL DO ACTION: ☐
AFTER PROGRAM: 0 ☐ 20% ☐ 40% ☐ 60% ☐ 80% ☐ 100% ☐

What percent of the time do you avoid burning wood when there is a smog alert in your community?

BEFORE PROGRAM: N/A ☐ 0 ☐ 20% ☐ 40% ☐ 60% ☐ 80% ☐ 100% ☐
WILL DO ACTION: ☐
AFTER PROGRAM: 0 ☐ 20% ☐ 40% ☐ 60% ☐ 80% ☐ 100% ☐

When you have a fire, what percent of the time do you use very dry wood or compressed sawdust logs or pellets?

BEFORE PROGRAM: N/A ☐ 0 ☐ 20% ☐ 40% ☐ 60% ☐ 80% ☐ 100% ☐
WILL DO ACTION: ☐
AFTER PROGRAM: 0 ☐ 20% ☐ 40% ☐ 60% ☐ 80% ☐ 100% ☐

What percent of the time do you use alternatives to outdoor burning such as chipping or composting?

BEFORE PROGRAM: N/A ☐ 0 ☐ 20% ☐ 40% ☐ 60% ☐ 80% ☐ 100% ☐
WILL DO ACTION: ☐
AFTER PROGRAM: 0 ☐ 20% ☐ 40% ☐ 60% ☐ 80% ☐ 100% ☐

15. FARTHER DOWN THE PATH: "A SUSTAINABLE ENERGY HOUSEHOLD" -
Achieving maximum energy efficiency

If your local electric utility offers a "green power" option (solar, hydro, wind, geothermal, biomass etc.) are you a subscriber?

BEFORE PROGRAM: ☐ Yes ☐ No
WILL DO ACTION: ☐
AFTER PROGRAM: ☐ Yes ☐ No

Have you installed any renewable energy systems in your home?

BEFORE PROGRAM: ☐ Yes ☐ No
WILL DO ACTION: ☐
AFTER PROGRAM: ☐ Yes ☐ No

If you have an attic, what percent of your attic or roof is insulated?

BEFORE PROGRAM: N/A ☐ 0 ☐ 20% ☐ 40% ☐ 60% ☐ 80% ☐ 100% ☐
WILL DO ACTION: ☐
AFTER PROGRAM: 0 ☐ 20% ☐ 40% ☐ 60% ☐ 80% ☐ 100% ☐

What percent of your walls are insulated?

BEFORE PROGRAM: N/A ☐ 0 ☐ 20% ☐ 40% ☐ 60% ☐ 80% ☐ 100% ☐
WILL DO ACTION: ☐
AFTER PROGRAM: 0 ☐ 20% ☐ 40% ☐ 60% ☐ 80% ☐ 100% ☐

Do you have a long-term plan for improving energy efficiency and converting to renewable resources in your home?

BEFORE PROGRAM: ☐ Yes ☐ No
WILL DO ACTION: ☐
AFTER PROGRAM: ☐ Yes ☐ No

To estimate your household's transportation habits, ask each member of your household who is participating on your EcoTeam to fill in a Transportation Tracker for one week. Collect each person's Tracker, compile their responses into a household total or average, and record these answers in the spaces provided below. Members will also fill in a Tracker at the end of the program to reflect changes in their transportation habits. Some questions in the transportation section require interviewing individual members of your household. You may wish to gather together and fill out these questions all at once or you can do these interviews one by one.

Questions requiring data from Interviews and Trackers have been labeled with one of these two symbols:

Tr = Transportation Tracker   Int = Interview

ACTIONS	BEFORE PROGRAM	WILL DO ACTION	AFTER PROGRAM
1. GETTING THERE ON YOUR OWN STEAM – *Walking and Biking*			
Has someone in your household researched alternative routes for human-powered modes of transportation to get to work and other regular destinations (bike, walk, roller blade)?	❑ Yes ❑ No	❑	❑ Yes ❑ No
How many miles in this week did participating members of your household use a human-powered mode of transportation? **Tr**	_____miles household **total**	❑	_____miles household **total**
How many weeks per year will this be done? **Tr**	_____ weeks household **average**	❑	_____ weeks household **average**

ACTIONS	BEFORE PROGRAM	WILL DO ACTION	AFTER PROGRAM

2. ENERGY X MASS -
   Using public transportation

Has someone in your household researched public transportation routes to common household destinations?

❑ Yes ❑ No   ❑   ❑ Yes ❑ No

How many miles in this week did participating members of your household use public transportation?   **Tr**

_____miles
household **total**
❑
_____miles
household **total**

How many weeks per year will this be done?   **Tr**

_____ weeks
household **average**
❑
_____ weeks
household **average**

3. A GOOD DEED - *Combining trips*

How many miles in this week did participating members of your household drive to a single destination and back (didn't combine trips)?   **Tr**

_____miles
household **total**
❑
_____miles
household **total**

Do people in your household regularly cluster errands that are in the same parts of town so that they minimize trips to single destinations and back?

❑ Yes ❑ No   ❑   ❑ Yes ❑ No

ACTIONS		BEFORE PROGRAM	WILL DO ACTION	AFTER PROGRAM

4. RELAX AND RIDE -
Carpooling

How many miles in this week did participating members of your household carpool? **Tr**

_____miles household **total** | ❑ | _____miles household **total**

How many of these miles were in one of your own household's cars? **Tr**

_____miles household **total** | ❑ | _____miles household **total**

How many miles in this week did participating members of your household drive "solo" (didn't carpool)? **Tr**

_____miles household **total** | ❑ | _____miles household **total**

5. THE ROAD NOT TAKEN -
Telecommuting/alternative work schedules

Household total of miles commuted to work weekly: **Tr**

_____miles household **total** | ❑ | _____miles household **total**

6. DRIVE EARTH SMART -
Developing fuel-efficient driving habits

Determine your household's average highway speed. **Int**

_____ mph household **average** | ❑ | _____ mph household **average**

Estimate the number of highway miles driven by each participating household member in a year. **Int**

_____miles household **total** | ❑ | _____miles household **total**

Estimate the weight, in pounds, of things you carry in your car regularly, other than passengers, such as tools, trash, etc. **Int**

_____pounds household **total** | ❑ | _____pounds household **total**

Put the initials of each driver in your household at the top of a column. Check the box in their column if they answered yes. Fill in the "WILL DO ACTION" column if anyone in your household is participating

ACTIONS		BEFORE PROGRAM				WILL DO ACTION	AFTER PROGRAM			
		Initials:					Initials:			
		Driver 1	Driver 2	Driver 3	Driver 4		Driver 1	Driver 2	Driver 3	Driver 4
Do you accelerate slowly to avoid wasting fuel?	Int	❑	❑	❑	❑	❑	❑	❑	❑	❑
Do you turn off your vehicle when idling for more than a minute (when a train is passing or in a drive-thru lane)?	Int	❑	❑	❑	❑	❑	❑	❑	❑	❑
When driving, do you usually take the most fuel-efficient route to work?	Int	❑	❑	❑	❑	❑	❑	❑	❑	❑
If your household has more than one vehicle, do you regularly choose to drive the most fuel-efficient model?	Int	❑	❑	❑	❑	❑	❑	❑	❑	❑

7. DON'T BE AN OIL DRIP -
Identifying and plugging oil leaks on your car, boat, motorcycle or RV

How many household vehicles have oil leaks?	Int	___ household **total**		❑	___ household **total**
How many vehicles with oil leaks have you fixed since being on your EcoTeam?	Int	___ household **total**		❑	___ household **total**

ACTIONS		BEFORE PROGRAM			WILL DO ACTION	AFTER PROGRAM		
		Veh. 1	Veh. 2	Veh. 3		Veh. 1	Veh. 2	Veh. 3

8. IS YOUR VEHICLE PHYSICALLY FIT? - *Tune-ups and maintenance for your vehicle*

ACTIONS		Veh. 1	Veh. 2	Veh. 3		Veh. 1	Veh. 2	Veh. 3
Check the box if this vehicle is on a regular maintenance schedule.	Int	❏	❏	❏	❏	❏	❏	❏
Check the box if this vehicle is due for a tune up.	Int	❏	❏	❏	❏			
If it needed one, did this vehicle get a tune-up since your EcoTeam began?	Int				❏	❏	❏	❏
Check this box if you check the air pressure in this vehicle's tires regularly.	Int	❏	❏	❏	❏	❏	❏	❏

9. BEFRIEND AN EARTH-SMART AUTO - *Researching and purchasing a fuel-efficient vehicle*

If you have purchased a fuel-efficient vehicle since participating on an EcoTeam, what is the new miles per gallon?

_____miles per gal
of new vehicle

ACTIONS	BEFORE PROGRAM	WILL DO ACTION	AFTER PROGRAM
Fuel economy and low emissions will be a high-priority in the next vehicle purchased by our household.	❑ Yes ❑ No	❑	❑ Yes ❑ No

10. VACATION WITH THE EARTH - *Fuel-efficient vacation planning*

Reducing the amount of fuel used for traveling on vacation is a high priority for our household.	❑ Yes ❑ No	❑	❑ Yes ❑ No

11. FARTHER DOWN THE PATH:
Finding alternatives to driving alone

Does your household have a plan for reducing the number of miles traveled in an automobile?	❑ Yes ❑ No	❑	❑ Yes ❑ No

By what percentage are you planning to reduce your household's single-occupancy vehicle miles traveled (driver alone)?	N/A 0 20% 40% 60% 80% 100% ❑ ❑ ❑ ❑ ❑ ❑ ❑	❑	0 20% 40% 60% 80% 100% ❑ ❑ ❑ ❑ ❑ ❑

ACTIONS	BEFORE PROGRAM	WILL DO ACTION	AFTER PROGRAM

1. VOTE FOR THE EARTH -
Choosing Earth-friendly products

How often do you choose products of highest quality because they last longer?

	N/A	0	20%	40%	60%	80%	100%		0	20%	40%	60%	80%	100%
	☐	☐	☐	☐	☐	☐	☐	☐	☐	☐	☐	☐	☐	☐

How often do you choose products with minimal recycled or recyclable packaging?

	N/A	0	20%	40%	60%	80%	100%		0	20%	40%	60%	80%	100%
	☐	☐	☐	☐	☐	☐	☐	☐	☐	☐	☐	☐	☐	☐

How often do you choose "Earth-friendly" products which are:

energy efficient?

	N/A	0	20%	40%	60%	80%	100%		0	20%	40%	60%	80%	100%
	☐	☐	☐	☐	☐	☐	☐	☐	☐	☐	☐	☐	☐	☐

biodegradable?

	N/A	0	20%	40%	60%	80%	100%		0	20%	40%	60%	80%	100%
	☐	☐	☐	☐	☐	☐	☐	☐	☐	☐	☐	☐	☐	☐

post-consumer or recycled material content?

	N/A	0	20%	40%	60%	80%	100%		0	20%	40%	60%	80%	100%
	☐	☐	☐	☐	☐	☐	☐	☐	☐	☐	☐	☐	☐	☐

locally made?

	N/A	0	20%	40%	60%	80%	100%		0	20%	40%	60%	80%	100%
	☐	☐	☐	☐	☐	☐	☐	☐	☐	☐	☐	☐	☐	☐

non-toxic?

	N/A	0	20%	40%	60%	80%	100%		0	20%	40%	60%	80%	100%
	☐	☐	☐	☐	☐	☐	☐	☐	☐	☐	☐	☐	☐	☐

ACTIONS	BEFORE PROGRAM	WILL DO ACTION	AFTER PROGRAM

2. THINK BEFORE YOU BUY -
Finding alternatives to recreational shopping and impulse buying

Do you practice alternatives to recreational shopping (relaxing, spending time with friends or family, gardening, etc.) and impulse buying (only shopping from a list, waiting a day before you buy)?

❑ Yes ❑ No   ❑   ❑ Yes ❑ No

How often do you make gifts rather than buy them?

N/A 0 20% 40% 60% 80% 100%
❑ ❑ ❑ ❑ ❑ ❑ ❑   ❑   0 20% 40% 60% 80% 100%
❑ ❑ ❑ ❑ ❑ ❑

3. TOXIC SLEUTH -
Reducing toxic products in your home

If you use toxic products, do you store them safely?

❑ Yes ❑ No   ❑   ❑ Yes ❑ No

How many toxic products have you replaced with non-toxic alternatives since your EcoTeam began?

#____ toxics replaced

4. A BREATH OF FRESH AIR -
Reducing the use of home products that contribute to air pollution

Do you use alternatives to products that come in aerosol cans?

❑ Yes ❑ No   ❑   ❑ Yes ❑ No

Do you use an alternative to lighter fluid to start your grill (charcoal chimney or electric starter)?

❑ Yes ❑ No   ❑   ❑ Yes ❑ No

When purchasing solvents, paints and cleaning materials, do you choose environmentally friendly alternatives?

❑ Yes ❑ No   ❑   ❑ Yes ❑ No

ACTIONS	BEFORE PROGRAM	WILL DO ACTION	AFTER PROGRAM

5. HOME SWEET HOME -
Choosing non-toxic furnishings and building materials for your home

When purchasing building materials and furnishings for your home, do you choose non-toxic and environmentally safe alternatives?

BEFORE PROGRAM: ☐ Yes ☐ No   WILL DO ACTION: ☐   AFTER PROGRAM: ☐ Yes ☐ No

6. WHAT GOES AROUND CAME AROUND -
Choosing recycled paper products

How frequently do you buy paper products made from recycled materials or post-consumer waste?

BEFORE PROGRAM: N/A 0 20% 40% 60% 80% 100% ☐ ☐ ☐ ☐ ☐ ☐ ☐
WILL DO ACTION: ☐
AFTER PROGRAM: 0 20% 40% 60% 80% 100% ☐ ☐ ☐ ☐ ☐ ☐

7. VEGETABLE SOUP -
Choosing organic produce

What percent of the produce that you buy is organic?

BEFORE PROGRAM: N/A 0 20% 40% 60% 80% 100% ☐ ☐ ☐ ☐ ☐ ☐ ☐
WILL DO ACTION: ☐
AFTER PROGRAM: 0 20% 40% 60% 80% 100% ☐ ☐ ☐ ☐ ☐ ☐

8. NEAR AND DEAR -
Choosing local produce and dairy

What percent of the produce that you eat is locally grown?

BEFORE PROGRAM: N/A 0 20% 40% 60% 80% 100% ☐ ☐ ☐ ☐ ☐ ☐ ☐
WILL DO ACTION: ☐
AFTER PROGRAM: 0 20% 40% 60% 80% 100% ☐ ☐ ☐ ☐ ☐ ☐

If you eat dairy, what percent is locally produced?

BEFORE PROGRAM: N/A 0 20% 40% 60% 80% 100% ☐ ☐ ☐ ☐ ☐ ☐ ☐
WILL DO ACTION: ☐
AFTER PROGRAM: 0 20% 40% 60% 80% 100% ☐ ☐ ☐ ☐ ☐ ☐

ACTIONS	BEFORE PROGRAM		WILL DO ACTION	AFTER PROGRAM	

9. CHEW ON THIS FOR AWHILE - *Increasing meatless meals*

How many meatless meals do your household members eat per week?

Name	# meatless meals		Name	# meatless meals
_____	_____		_____	_____
_____	_____	☐	_____	_____
_____	_____		_____	_____
_____	_____		_____	_____
_____	_____		_____	_____
_____	_____		_____	_____
HH Total: _____			HH Total: _____	

DOESN'T THIS LOOK YUMMY?

WOW

YEE-HAW!

THE VEGETARIAN GOURMET

YEAH!

10. SWAP PARTY- *Exchanging items instead of throwing them away*

Do you swap goods, such as household items, clothing or furniture?

☐ Yes ☐ No   ☐   ☐ Yes ☐ No

11. LOAN ON ME - *Loaning and borrowing items with neighbors*

Do you use a "loan and borrow" system for tools or other items you don't need often?

☐ Yes ☐ No   ☐   ☐ Yes ☐ No

12. WHEN THE "GOTTA HAVE ITS" ATTACK, HEAD FOR THE GARDEN - *Growing your own food*

If you garden, how much of your household's food do you produce?

N/A 0 20% 40% 60% 80% 100%   0 20% 40% 60% 80% 100%
☐ ☐ ☐ ☐ ☐ ☐ ☐   ☐   ☐ ☐ ☐ ☐ ☐ ☐

ACTIONS	BEFORE PROGRAM	WILL DO ACTION	AFTER PROGRAM

13. A GREEN GARDENER - *Reducing the use of toxic pesticides.*

Do you use pest and drought-resistant native plants for your garden?

☐ Yes ☐ No   ☐   ☐ Yes ☐ No

Do you handle unwelcome pests without using toxic pesticides?

☐ Yes ☐ No   ☐   ☐ Yes ☐ No

14. FARTHER DOWN THE PATH - *Improving your quality of life through non-materialistic means*

Do you have a plan for improving the quality of your life through activities that don't rely heavily on the consumption of natural resources?

☐ Yes ☐ No   ☐   ☐ Yes ☐ No

How many hours a month have you committed to these quality-of-life activities?

_____ # hours/month

ASSESSMENT NOTES

PROGRAM SUPPORT TOOLS

INTRODUCTION

This section provides a support structure to help you effectively implement the program. It includes:

Team Initiator Guidelines: A 5-step process for starting your team.

Information Meeting Guide: A script for conducting an informational meeting for potential team members. It's also possible to use this guide for one-on-one communications.

Team Building Meeting Guide: A script for conducting the first team meeting. This team can consist of household members or 5 to 8 friends, neighbors, colleagues, or faith community members. The focus of the meeting is to review each of the program elements, build a team, schedule the remaining meetings, and choose people to lead them.

Topic Meeting Guide: This script is used for meetings 2 through 7. The goal in these meetings is for team participants to report on actions taken, describe action plans for the next section, and get support from their team.

Carry Over Actions: This enables you to keep track of actions you have committed to take but have not completed.

Team Members and Schedule: This enables you to have team members, contact information and the dates of future meetings in one easy-to-find location.

Team Initiator Guidelines

1. If you are starting the team, you are the team initiator. To learn about the program, read the introduction, how the program works, the table of contents and review the actions.

2. Set a date and time for hosting a Team Building Meeting either in your home or at some other location.

3. Create your team. This can consist of family, friends, neighbors, co-workers, or members of your faith community or civic organization. Choose the community that is easiest to pull together. The best size for a team is 5-8 households. If that is not possible, your household unit can become the team. If potential team members wish to know more about the program, invite them to visit www.empowermentinstitute.net/glh.

4. Each household will need to have a copy of this book. It can be purchased on-line at www.empowermentinstitute.net/glh. Books can also be purchased from Amazon.com, or your local bookstore.

5. As the team initiator you are responsible for leading the Team Building Meeting. The following meetings will be divided among the rest of the team members. Meeting scripts are located in this section.

INFORMATION MEETING GUIDE

BEFORE EVENT

○ If possible, serve light refreshments and set up room in a U shape to increase sense of intimacy.

○ Review this script before the meeting so that you are familiar with the process.

AGENDA (Times Approximate)

1. Welcome, Purpose, Agenda - 10 minutes
2. Introductions - 15 minutes
3. Overview of Challenge - 15 minutes
4. Program Description - 10 minutes
5. Q & A - 15 minutes
6. Invitation to Participate - 10 minutes
7. Sign-up - 15 minutes
Total Time: 90 minutes

1. WELCOME, PURPOSE, AGENDA – 10 MINUTES

○ Welcome: Welcome and appreciate people for coming. State your name and role as the team initiator.

○ Purpose: To provide an opportunity to live a more environmentally sustainable lifestyle. Include your personal motivation for organizing this event.

○ Agenda: Introductions, overview of challenge, program description, Q & A, invitation to participate.

2. INTRODUCTIONS – 15 MINUTES

○ Invite participants to state name, where they live, and any other important information and to say what they would like out of the meeting. If a large group limit the sharing to 8-10 people.

3. OVERVIEW – 15 MINUTES

○ Read out key points from page 1.

○ Ask people to talk about what they've done already to create a more environmentally sustainable lifestyle

○ Ask people to talk about what more they would like to do.

○ Ask them what has gotten in the way.

4. PROGRAM DESCRIPTION – 10 MINUTES

○ Show copy of this book and read "How the Program Works"

5. Q & A – 15 MINUTES

○ Invite questions about the program and their participation. Draw out any concerns that individuals might have about participation.

6. INVITATION TO PARTICIPATE ON A TEAM – 10 MINUTES

○ Ask how many are interested in participating in the program? Acknowledge those that raise their hand and draw out any concerns from those who didn't. For those who can't join now, invite them to do the program on their own or join a team in the future.

○ Invite participants to spread the word to others and have them contact you if they wish to participate on a team. Provide your name, e-mail, and phone number on a flip chart if available.

7. TEAM PROGRAM SIGN UP AND PLACEMENT – 15 MINUTES

○ If several teams are formed, organize in groups of 5-8 households by proximity, affinity, or other criteria.

○ All can meet at one location and then divide up into sub-groups of 5-8 households or can divide up into separate teams. In either case, request a volunteer from each team to serve as team leader. Point them to the scripts starting on page 144 of the book that tell them how to lead the meetings.

○ Set date(s) for the Team Building Meeting.

TEAM BUILDING MEETING GUIDE

BEFORE THE MEETING

○ Review this guide before the meeting so you are familiar with the process.

○ Review *Green Living Handbook* with emphasis on "How the Program Works" and the "Sustainable Lifestyle Assessment."

○ Fill out the Garbage Section of the Sustainable Lifestyle Assessment.

AGENDA (Times Approximate)

1. Welcome, Purpose, Overview - 15 minutes
2. Participants State Reasons for Joining - 20 minutes
3. Review How Program Works - 10 minutes
4. Review the Sustainable Lifestyle Assessment - 10 minutes
5. Review Workbook and Action Plan - 20 minutes
6. Schedule Meetings - 15 minutes
7. Next Steps - 5 minutes
Total Time - 1.5 to 2 Hours

1. WELCOME, PURPOSE, OVERVIEW – 15 MINUTES

○ Welcome participants and thank them for coming. State why you were motivated to form this team.

○ Indicate that the purpose of this meeting is to review each of the program elements, build a team, schedule the remaining meetings and choose people to lead them.

○ Review highlights from the introduction to the book on page 1.

2. PARTICIPANTS STATE REASONS FOR PARTICIPATING – 20 MINUTES

○ Ask team members to state their name, where they live (if relevant), and why they chose to participate.

○ Write down why each person chose to participate.

○ At the end, summarize the key reasons individuals chose to participate. Create into a team statement of purpose. Invite team members to write this on the page before the Table of Contents in their handbook.

3. REVIEW HOW PROGRAM WORKS – 10 MINUTES

○ Review seven points on page 2.

4. REVIEW THE SUSTAINABLE LIFESTYLE ASSESSMENT (SLA) – 10 MINUTES

○ Ask everyone to turn to Page 109.

○ Share what you learned from filling out the garbage section of the SLA and your action plan.

○ Review the guidelines.

○ Answer any questions people may have about filling out the SLA.

5. REVIEW HANDBOOK AND ACTION LOGS – 20 MINUTES

○ Invite participants to review the actions in the Table of Contents to familiarize themselves with the program content.

○ Review the Garbage Action Log in beginning of the section.

○ Select one of the actions and review the format.

○ Answer any questions.

6. SCHEDULE MEETINGS – 15 MINUTES

○ Schedule the topic meetings, allowing 10 -14 days between meetings for taking the actions.

○ Explain that there is a topic meeting script located on page 147. Ask for volunteers to lead each of the remaining meetings.

○ Have team members enter meeting dates and times and each other's phone/e-mail addresses on page 151 of their *Green Living Handbook*.

○ Request that everyone commit to coming on time and the meeting ending on time. If something unexpected occurs and someone cannot attend a meeting, request that the person notify the topic leader in advance and provide their action plan. The topic leader will call them after the meeting to explain what happened.

7. REVIEW NEXT STEPS – 5 MINUTES

○ Read the Garbage Chapter.

○ Fill in the "Before Program" and "Will Do" columns of the Sustainable Lifestyle Assessment.

○ Transfer your "Will Do" actions to the Garbage Action Log in the beginning of that chapter.

TOPIC MEETING GUIDE

BEFORE THE MEETING

○ Read next chapter.

○ Review this Topic Meeting Guide.

○ Collect any local information relevant for taking actions in this chapter.

○ Select and take the actions you wish to demonstrate.

○ Plan how you will lead steps 1, 3, and 4.

○ Fill in the "Before Program" and "Will Do" columns of the Sustainable Lifestyle Assessment for this chapter.

○ Transfer your "Will Do" actions to the Action Log in the beginning of the chapter.

AGENDA (Times Approximate)

1. Inspirational Start - 5 minutes
2. Discuss Sustainable Lifestyle Assessment - 20 minutes
3. Provide local information for taking actions, do demonstrations and share your action log - 10 minutes
4. Team members share Action Logs and get support - 20 minutes
5. Check in on Team Performance - 10 minutes
6. Set Up Support Calls - 5 minutes
7. Review Next Steps - 5 minutes
8. Acknowledge Team's Accomplishments - 10 minutes
Total Time 1.5 - 2 hours

1. INSPIRATIONAL START – 5 MINUTES

○ Start with a brief poem, quote, personal anecdote, or something that connects the group to the meaning and larger purpose of what you are doing.

2. DISCUSS THE SUSTAINABLE LIFESTYLE ASSESSMENT – 20 MINUTES

○ What did I learn?

○ Were there any big surprises?

○ Is there anything I am proud of?

○ Where do I need to make improvements?

3. PROVIDE LOCAL INFORMATION FOR TAKING ACTIONS, DO DEMONSTRATIONS AND SHARE YOUR ACTION LOG – 10 MINUTES

○ Distribute local information.

○ Do demonstrations of selected actions you have completed. Describe what you did and how you did it so the team can learn from your hands-on experience. Show any of the materials you are using.

○ Share the rest of your Action Log with the team. Be sure to give the time and day you plan to do the actions. This models careful planning.

4. TEAM MEMBERS SHARE ACTION LOGS AND GET SUPPORT – 20 MINUTES

○ Summarize each action for your teammates and ask who plans to take it.

○ Have team members who would like support in taking a particular action ask other team members for help.

○ Plan joint actions as desired. These are activities where two or more households work together outside of the meeting to complete an action.

5. CHECK IN ON TEAM PERFORMANCE – 10 MINUTES

○ At each meeting, the team is encouraged to review their process. The purpose is to look at how the team is doing and address any issues so they don't grow into problems. Ask the following questions.

○ *Was anyone missing from the meeting?* If so, give that person a call and review what happened at the meeting.

○ *Did everyone come on time?* Teams have different personalities. Some are very business oriented and they like to start on time, move through the agenda, and complete the meeting in an efficient way. Other teams are more social and time is less of a factor. It is important to explore this as a team so no one is frustrated.

○ *Did each person fill in his or her action logs?* If some people didn't do this, explain that this is the foundation for taking action and ask if everyone will agree to complete their Action Log for the next meeting.

○ *How are we doing as a team?* Invite people to express successes, concerns, or ways they could use support.

6. SET UP SUPPORT CALLS – 5 MINUTES

○ Approximately half way between this meeting and the next, you as team leader are encouraged to call team members to see how they are doing in implementing their action plans. Left on our own, our motivation often wanes. These support calls make a big difference in assisting team members to stay on track.

○ Arrange mutually convenient times for checking in with team members. Allow up to 10 minutes per call. If person is not there for the agreed upon call, leave a message and request a call back with a status report.

7. REVIEW NEXT STEPS – 5 MINUTES

○ Take the planned actions.

○ Read the next chapter.

○ Fill in the "Before Program" and "Will Do" columns of the Sustainable Lifestyle Assessment for the next topic.

○ Transfer the "Will Do" column to the Action Log and make your plan.

○ Determine any support you desire from the team to complete the action(s) in your plan.

8. ACKNOWLEDGE TEAM'S ACCOMPLISHMENTS – 10 MINUTES

○ Express your appreciation to team members for what they have accomplished. State in a sentence or two what was most meaningful for you and invite others to do the same. If appropriate, end with some type of celebration.

CARRY OVER ACTIONS

Write the actions below that you intend to complete.

Action	Page #	Target Date	Notes

ECOTEAM MEMBERS AND SCHEDULE

Please complete all information.

Session	Meeting Date/Time	Meeting Location	Topic Leader
1. Team Building			
2. Garbage			
3. Water			
4. Energy			
5. Transportation			
6. Consumption			
7. Empowering Others			
8. Introduction Event (optional)			

TEAM MEMBERS:

1. Name: _____ Address: _____
    Phone—Home: _____ Work: _____ E-mail: _____

2. Name: _____ Address: _____
    Phone—Home: _____ Work: _____ E-mail: _____

3. Name: _____ Address: _____
    Phone—Home: _____ Work: _____ E-mail: _____

4. Name: _____ Address: _____
    Phone—Home: _____ Work: _____ E-mail: _____

5. Name: _____ Address: _____
    Phone—Home: _____ Work: _____ E-mail: _____

6. Name: _____ Address: _____
    Phone—Home: _____ Work: _____ E-mail: _____

7. Name: _____ Address: _____
    Phone—Home: _____ Work: _____ E-mail: _____

8. Name: _____ Address: _____
    Phone—Home: _____ Work: _____ E-mail: _____

9. Name: _____ Address: _____
    Phone—Home: _____ Work: _____ E-mail: _____

10. Name: _____ Address: _____
    Phone—Home: _____ Work: _____ E-mail: _____

11. Name: _____ Address: _____
    Phone—Home: _____ Work: _____ E-mail: _____

12. Name: _____ Address: _____
    Phone—Home: _____ Work: _____ E-mail: _____

ABOUT THE AUTHOR

David Gershon, founder and CEO of Empowerment Institute, is one of the world's leading authorities on behavior change and large-scale transformation. He applies his expertise to various issues requiring community, organizational, or societal transformation. His clients range from large cities and organizations to social entrepreneurs and transformational small businesses. He has addressed issues ranging from environmental behavior change to emergency preparedness; from organizational talent development to low-income neighborhood revitalization. Longitudinal research studies indicate that adopted behavior changes are sustained over time.

He conceived and organized, in partnership with the United Nations Children's Fund and ABC Television, one of the planet's first major global initiatives, the First Earth Run. At the height of the Cold War, using the mythic power of relaying fire around the world, millions of people, in partnership with the world's political leaders and media, participated in creating a profound sense of our connectedness.

David is the author of nine books including *Low Carbon Diet: A 30 Day Program to Lose 5000 Pounds*, and the bestselling *Empowerment: The Art of Creating Your Life As You Want It*, which has become a classic on the subject. He is currently writing *Social Change 2.0 - Unleashing Social Creativity and the New Practice of Empowerment*. Considered a master personal development trainer, he co-directs the Empowerment Institute Certification Program, a school for transformative change. He has lectured at Harvard, MIT, and Duke and served as an advisor to the Clinton White House and United Nations on behavior change and sustainability issues. His work has received considerable media attention and many honors.

OTHER PROGRAMS AND BOOKS BY DAVID GERSHON

Low Carbon Diet: A 30 Day Program to Lose 5000 Pounds—Grounded in over two decades of environmental behavior change research, this illustrated workbook offers readers much more than a to-do list of eco-friendly actions. With practicality and humor, bestselling author and environmental change pioneer David Gershon walks readers through every step of the carbon-reduction process, from calculating their current CO_2 footprint to tracking their progress and measuring their impact. By making simple changes to actions they take every day, readers learn how to reduce their annual household CO_2 output by at least 15%. And, for those who are more ambitious, there are chapters on how to help one's workplace, local schools, and community do the same. For more information visit www.empowermentinstitute.net/lcd.

Cool Community Campaign—The Cool Community Campaign engages local organizations across all sectors (including government, environmental organizations, businesses, neighborhood associations, faith-based groups, service clubs, and educational institutions) in a two-year campaign to engage up to 85% of the citizenry in *Low Carbon Diet's* proven program for household CO_2-reduction. The goal of the initiative is to help community residents reduce their carbon-footprint 20%. The first communities to achieve this goal will also serve as prototypes for the many cities and towns throughout America and around the world who are seeking effective climate change solutions. For more information visit www.empowermentinstitute.net/lcd.

Water Stewardship: A 30 Day Program to Protect and Conserve Our Water Resources—This program is designed to help neighborhoods and communities that are challenged by water quality or water conservation issues. It helps households develop practices to reduce their impact on local water bodies and conserve water in droughts. It can be done either as an individual household or a team. For more information visit www.empowermentinstitute.net.

Livable Neighborhood Program: Making Life Better on the Street Where You Live—This program has been successfully used in many communities to help neighbors improve the quality of life on their block. The action format is similar to *Green Living Handbook* but it is done as a team rather than an individual household. The program is divided into four sections: neighborhood health and safety, neighborhood beautification and greening, neighborhood resource sharing, and neighborhood community building. For more information visit www.empowermentinstitute.net.

All Together Now: Neighbors Helping Neighbors Create a Disaster Resilient Community—This program helps residents prepare for natural disasters, terrorist incidents, emergencies, or an avian flu pandemic. It uses the same action format as *Green Living Handbook* and is done either as a team or single household. It is designed to create disaster resilient blocks and buildings. For more information visit www.empowermentinstitute.net.

Journey for the Planet: A Kid's Five Week Adventure to Create an Earth Friendly Life—This is the children's version of the *Green Living Handbook*. It can be done by children on their own or as part of a classroom or youth group. A teacher's curriculum is available for use in the classroom. This program is described in the "A Down to Earth Family" action of the *Green Living Handbook*. For more information visit www.empowermentinstitute.net/journey.

Empowerment Institute Certification Program—Over the past 25 years, Empowerment Institute has developed highly effective transformational social change programs. It certifies leaders in all of the above programs in using these transformational and community empowerment tools. For more information visit www.empowermentinstitute.net.

Changing the World: The Craft of Transformative Leadership—This two-day training provides skills and inspiration for leaders implementing transformative change in an organization or community. It is customized for organizations or communities. For more information visit www.empowermentinstitute.net.

Dream for Our World—This book tells the mythic story of the First Earth Run and provides 7 practices that grew out of it for changing the world. For more information visit www.empowermentinstitute.net.

Empowerment: The Art of Creating Your Life As You Want It—Now in its 11th printing, and translated into eight languages, *Empowerment: The Art of Creating Your Life As You Want It* is widely considered to be a classic in the field of personal empowerment and transformation. Based on David Gershon and Gail Straub's two decades of work helping thousands of people create the life of their dreams, the book guides readers step-by-step through a systematic self-transformation program addressing seven key areas of life: relationships, sexuality, money, work, body, emotions, and spirituality. Its simple premise—that our thoughts and beliefs create the conditions of our life—is illustrated with anecdotes from each of the seven areas. Readers are then given practical and immediately applicable tools to help envision and create what they wish to achieve in each of these areas.

To order copies of any of the books listed, go to: www.empowermentinstitute.net